ORIGIN OF NAMES IN PECKHAM AND NUNHEAD

By John D. Beasley

Published by South Riding Press,
6 Everthorpe Road, London SE15 4DA
Fax and Telephone: 081-693 9412

Printed by LPL Print Service,
14 Castle Street, Bridgwater, Somerset TA6 3DB
Tel: 0278 429738   Fax: 0278 424043

TO
WALTER FINCH
WHOSE INFLUENCE SPREAD
FAR BEYOND PECKHAM

FOREWORD
by
Tessa Jowell
Member of Parliament for Dulwich

Dulwich means "the meadow where dill grows", while Peckham means village by a hill – probably Nunhead Hill. Nunhead is a local name with particularly gruesome origins. At first "Nonehead", Elizabethan England recorded this name after a Mother Superior was beheaded for opposing Henry VIII's pitiless sacking of the monasteries. Her severed head was placed on a pike for public view at Nunhead Green. King John was believed to have killed a stag while hunting in Peckham; hence the King John pub in Peckham High Street.

John Beasley is a prolific local historian and writer who shares his evident love of Peckham and Nunhead with us. This catalogue of local place names and their history is clearly a project motivated by fascination and an evangelism which wants to ensure that others with similar curiosity will be similarly well informed.

It shows a dedication to home and neighbourhood that is rare in London now, where people move on usually without the opportunity to put down roots or to develop the curiosity which gives expression to attachment to neighbourhood.

This book catalogues street and place names. It also covers the origin of pub names and more recent local shops. It reminds us that Peckham and Nunhead were developed in two stages. Most of the early development was comfortably Victorian. The later development started in the late 1930's and continued with the development of pre- and post-war housing estates. Small terraces of cottages which stood under their own names were gradually parcelled up and renamed as Bellenden Road, Consort Road, Ondine Road and so on.

I expected to dip into this book, but in fact I read it from beginning to end. It has added to my curiosity about this special part of London, which it is such a privilege to represent in Parliament. I look forward to John's next volume.

AUTHOR'S PREFACE

Abraham Lincoln admitted: "I have changed my mind and I don't think much of a man who isn't wiser today than he was yesterday." This book would not have been written if I had not changed my mind.

L. S. Sherwood compiled "Camberwell Place and Street Names and Their Origin" which was typed and issued by Camberwell Borough Council in 1964.

It was obvious that the work Mr. Sherwood did on Peckham names needed updating and expanding, but I felt that a book on the origin of names in Peckham and Nunhead would leave too many questions unanswered.

By courtesy *South London Press*

Her Royal Highness The Princess Margaret arriving to open The Aylesham Centre.

However, I decided to write the book through seeing an Aylesham Centre sign in Hanover Park as I drove to work at 7.20 a.m. on 16 July 1986. Though I didn't like the name of the new shopping centre I felt that people had the right to know why it was so called. Then followed a fascinating search for the origins of over 800 names in SE15.

I owe a great debt to Leslie Sherwood for his research. Though he lived at 138 Copleston Road, close to my home, I never met him but did receive a letter from him in 1981 when he was 82. He described his research as "a very absorbing job, completed just before my retirement in 1964".

It has not been possible to check all Leslie Sherwood's sources. Some origins may be inspired guesswork. A few errors have been corrected.

Many primary sources have been impossible to find because information was destroyed or not recorded; some may be hidden in the *South London Press* and other local newspapers which are not indexed.

Some records were destroyed after the Greater London Council was abolished so the origins of certain names used in the last twenty years cannot be traced.

Dates given for streets built in the 19th century are as published in London County Council records but are not necessarily the dates on which streets were built.

In *The Streets of London*[1] Sheila Fairfield wrote: "At times of rapid expansion, particularly in south and north-west London, streets rolled out like matting in all directions, and dozens of names were needed all at once. Anything would do that sounded pleasant: lists of English towns, Scottish lochs, holiday resorts, great rivers and famous peaks were all pressed into service from 1850 onwards. They had no local relevance at all; they were a kind of topographical formica."

Achievement: A Short History of the London County Council[2] stated: "When London was a small city surrounded by a wall and a number of isolated villages it was understandable that each community should have a High Street, or a Church Street, or a George Street or a James Street (called after the king of the day). When London had coalesced into one great metropolis there was, in consequence, great duplication and repetition of street names through the area. There were dozens and dozens of streets with similar names. The Board of Works had, in its time, changed the names of over 3,000. The Council, prodded by the Post Office, carried out a programme of renaming, and by 1935 had altered another 2,700 street names. In 1935 it decided to abolish all duplicate street names in the County. There were then nearly 4,000 of them. One of the headaches was to find acceptable new names. Old maps were consulted, old field names were revived, and historical and local associations were made use of."

What may surprise many readers is that some recent names have no local connections. Shakespeare and Shelley had no links with Peckham but properties have been named after them in the last few years. Southwark Council has a list of well-known people from which names are selected. Telephone directories have been used in the same way.

Flats on the North Peckham Estate were named after places in Hampshire; some are now in Dorset because of boundary changes. There is a link with nearby Southampton Way built on land owned by the D'Uvedales whose principal estates were in Hampshire.

The Gloucester Grove Estate has blocks named after places in the former county of Gloucestershire; some are now in Avon.

Where names include "The", such as The Aylesham Centre and various pubs, this has been omitted.

A few names have ceased to be used since research for the book began e.g. Claudia Jones Youth Club.

Many people have assisted by providing information and making useful suggestions. I am grateful to them all. Special thanks must go to Doug Baker, Marian Beasley, Carol Harrison, Stephen Humphrey, Stephen Potter, Carol Quamina, Nicola Smith and Ron Woollacott.

I also greatly appreciate the foreword written by Tessa Jowell.

The book is dedicated to Walter Finch (1919-1991) who was born in Burchell Road, was actively involved in Peckham Methodist Church for over sixty years, trained as a microbiologist and became Vice Principal of Paddington College. He was chairman of the Institute of Medical Laboratory Technology. After retiring he became a governor at Waverley School and was elected as chair. His untimely death is still keenly felt by his many friends.

Walter Finch suggested that I should write a book to mark the centenary of the South London Mission so *The Bitter Cry Heard and Heeded* was published.

Walter Finch proposed the name Cherry Tree Court for the new flats on the site of the former Queen's Road Methodist Church opened in 1865 and demolished in 1972. If the origin of every name in SE15 had been as well recorded as Cherry Tree Court this book would be comprehensive.

I hope readers will provide missing information and point out any errors. All material sent to me will be deposited in Southwark Local Studies Library, 211 Borough High Street, SE1 1JA (071-403 3507) where much research for this book was done. Many lunch hours were spent in Bethnal Green Reference Library doing basic research and writing.

As I travel outside SE15 I am intrigued by other names. Every district needs a book giving the origin of its names. I hope this volume will inspire other local historians, in the London Borough of Southwark and other parts of Britain, to compile similar books.

Peckham, 1993 J.D.B.

[1] *The Streets of London: A dictionary of the names and their origins* by Sheila Fairfield. Papermac, 1984.

[2] *Achievement: A Short History of the London County Council* by W. Eric Jackson. Longmans, 1965.

KEY

(B) Business premises

(P) Pub

(e.g. Warburton Road) Indicates either the former name of the road or the names of individual terraces or houses or former names of parts of road.

[ ] Key to sources and further reading. See page 87.

A

ABBEY NATIONAL, 97 Rye Lane (B) National Building Society, formed in 1849, and Abbey Road Building Society, which began in 1874, merged in 1944. The branch in Rye Lane was opened in 1971. [310, 311]

ABBEY ROSE, Blackpool Road (B) Founder of Abbey Rose, Gwyn Reid Thomas, bought the bankrupt business of Abbott Iles & Co. in 1902. There were premises at Canal Head at that time. Mr. Thomas renamed the business Abbey Rose because he was keen on churches and flowers, and ABB starts most listings. The firm moved to Blackpool Road in 1988. [250, 251]

ABBOTSBURY MEWS, Nunhead Grove 1989 Abbotsbury in Dorset. [5, 344]

ABERDARE HOUSE, Sumner Estate 1951 Aberdare Canal. [1, 2, 12, 18]

ACORN ESTATE 1963 Camberwell Borough Council built Acorn Estate on the site of Acorn Place (1872). Previously the houses had been known as Emily's Cottages, Leonard's Cottages, End Cottages, Marsh's Cottages, Acorn Cottages and Mary's Terrace. Rose Cottages became part of Acorn Place in 1899. [7, 11, 14]

ACORN PARADE, Acorn Estate 1963 Fruit of the oak. [1, 14, 19]

ACORN WHARF, Frensham Street 1855 Timber importer Richard May acquired his premises at the side of the Grand Surrey Canal which he appropriately named Acorn Wharf. See *Who Who Was in Peckham.* [17, 36, 146]

ADYS ROAD 1878 (Warburton Road, Ravensdale Terrace, Rollistone Terrace, Oakover Terrace, Casterton Terrace, Lockington Terrace) John Adye, legal adviser to Edward Alleyn. In his diary Alleyn recorded that he dined with John Adye of Southwark on 22 September 1619. [1, 7, 10, 165]

ALDER CLOSE, North Peckham Estate Daniel Alder, landowner. Alder Street was built in 1863 and demolished when the North Peckham Estate was built. It was off Sumner Road south of Davey Street. [12, 20, 190]

ALDERHOLT WAY, North Peckham Estate 1971 Alderholt in Dorset. [2, 5, 12, 15, 22]

ALDER HOUSE, North Peckham Estate 1950 See Alder Close. [2, 12]

ALLIANCE, 260 Sumner Road (P) Shown on an 1870 map. Origin not traced. [296]

ALL SAINTS' CHURCH, Blenheim Grove Consecrated on 24 July 1872. All Saints' Day (1 November) is a feast to celebrate all the Christian saints, known and unknown. [3, 284]

ALMOND CLOSE, Atwell Estate 1964 Almond tree. [2]

ALMONDSBURY COURT, Gloucester Grove Estate 1975 Almondsbury in Avon. [2, 5]

ALPHA STREET Reputed to be the first street built in the Choumert Road district. Alpha is the first letter in the Greek alphabet. [1]

ALYS COURT, Blenheim Grove c. 1985 Origin not traced. [322]

AMBLESIDE POINT, Tustin Estate 1965 Ambleside in Cumbria. [2, 5, 14]

AMMON, 40 Sumner Road This residential home for elderly people was named after Lord Ammon (1873-1960) who was Labour M.P. for North Camberwell (1922-31 and 1935-44). The home was opened by one of his daughters, Miss Ada Ammon, M.B.E., on 20 March 1971. [38, 39, 58, 59]

AMOTT ROAD 1876 John Amott or Amyott was a friend of John Allen, Master of Dulwich College in the 1830s. [1, 7, 10]

AMSTEL COURT, Garnies Close 1971 River Amstel, Netherlands. Presumably because of Camberwell Borough Council's (and Southwark Borough Council's from 1965) friendship link with Deventer in the Netherlands. [26, 361, 410]

ANDOVERSFORD COURT, Gloucester Grove Estate 1977 Andoversford in Gloucestershire. [2, 5, 12]

ANGELINA HOUSE, Oliver Goldsmith Estate 1958 *Edwin and Angelina,* a ballad by Oliver Goldsmith written in 1764 and included in *The Vicar of Wakefield.* [1, 2, 23]

ANSDELL ROAD 1872 Probably Richard Ansdell (1815-85), animal painter. [1, 6, 7]

ANSTEY ROAD 1872 Anstey in Leicestershire or poet Christopher Anstey (1724-1805). A monument to him is in Poets' Corner in Westminster Abbey. [1, 5, 6, 7]

APOSTOLIC FAITH CHURCH, 95 Fenham Road This international evangelistic organisation holds to the teachings and practices of the Apostles and has for its motto: "Earnestly contend for the faith which was once delivered unto the saints" (Jude 3). [387]

APPLEGARTH HOUSE, Friary Estate 1952 Applegarth Town, in Dumfries and Galloway, where there was a monastery. [1, 5, 173]

ARCHERS WALK, Camden Estate 1976 Archer's Row was nearby in the 19th century. [2, 7, 400]

ARGOS, 54 Rye Lane (B) Opened on 15 November 1991 in part of the former premises of Marks and Spencer. According to *The Collins English Dictionary* "argosy" was "a large abundantly laden merchant ship, or a fleet of such ships". According to Greek mythology, Jason sailed out in the "Argo" in search of the treasured Golden Fleece. The name was picked from a list of suggested names for the catalogue store chain by Richard Tomkins, the company's founder; the company began trading under the name in 1973. [239, 246]

ARNOLD DOBSON HOUSE, St. Mary's Road 1978 Arnold Dobson was born in Preston in 1882 and came to London with his parents in about 1890. He went to Camberwell in 1892 and lived in Peckham Park Road until his marriage to Miss Elsie Swannell in 1921 when they moved to 285 Upland Road.

When he left Albany Road School, he worked first for a grocery company delivering tea by horse and cart, and then as a park attendant for Camberwell Borough Council on the newly opened One Tree Hill. After studying and passing his examinations, he joined the staff of the Borough Engineer's Department. In the First World War he served with the field ambulance section of the RASC in France, Salonika, Palestine and Egypt.

After the War he turned to Public Health and was appointed Sanitary Inspector in the Old Kent Road district.

The Second World War brought him varied duties as an ARP instructor, billeting and rehousing officer, home guard and fire-watcher as well as supplying his family with the produce of his allotment.

When he retired in 1948, his interests broadened in several ways. He was appointed to the East London Rent Tribunal, joined the Family Welfare Association, of which he was vice president. He took a special interest in the Camberwell Housing Society which was responsible for the Troy Town flats and social centre.

He became a manager of three schools. He also worked part-time for Thomas Cook's. He became a registered London Guide and acted as a courier from time to time on weekly coach tours.

After his wife died in 1961 Arnold Dobson enjoyed several overseas holidays including one to Canada and the U.S.A. Arnold Dobson took a lively interest in all these activities until the last two years of his life when he was housebound until his death on 5 September 1980. [2, 84, 85, 86]

ASHDENE, Acorn Estate 1962 Ash tree. Dene means vale. [1, 2, 14, 19]

ASTBURY ROAD 1874 (York Terrace) Probably after the Cheshire village of Astbury. [1, 5, 7]

ASYLUM ROAD 1867 (Bath Road) The Licensed Victuallers' Asylum (now Caroline Gardens) situated in that road. [1, 4, 7, 11]

ASYLUM TAVERN, 40 Asylum Road (P) See Asylum Road. [3]

ATHENLAY ROAD 1886 Ath = a ford; Lay = old form of lea i.e. meadow. [7, 350]

ATWELL ESTATE 1963 See Atwell Road. The estate was built on the sites of Atwell Road and Atwell Street (1879). [7, 14, 21]

ATWELL HOUSE See Atwell Road.

ATWELL ROAD 1864 (Rose Cottages) Hugh Atwell (or Attawel or Attewell) actor who was a member of Edward Alleyn's company, d. 1621. [1, 6, 7]

AUSTIN'S, 11-23 Peckham Rye (B) George Austin. See *Who Was Who in Peckham.* [17]

AVINGTON WAY, North Peckham Estate 1971 Avington in Hampshire. [2, 5, 12, 15]

AVONDALE RISE 1873 (Avondale Road; previously Gothic Villas, Cambridge Villas, Merrow Cottages, Anchor Villas, Harefield Villas, Osman Cottages, Yaxley Villas, Seaton Terrace, Gilbert Villas, Clarence Terrace, Girard Terrace, Walmer Villas.) Probably Lord Evandale in Sir Walter Scott's novel *Old Mortality.* [1, 7, 23]

AYLESBURY HOUSE, Friary Estate 1939 Franciscan community at Aylesbury in Buckinghamshire. [5, 14, 37, 361]

AYLESHAM CENTRE Kent mining village. Commemorates the link between Southwark Council and Aylesham during the miners' strike (1984-85). The Peckham Society wanted the shopping centre to be called the Thomas Tilling Centre. Princess Margaret opened The Aylesham Centre on 21 July 1988. [33, 34, 301]

AYRE, J. F. See J. F. Ayre.

AZENBY ROAD 1868 (Azenby Road, Aylmer Road, Aspenlow Terrace, Azenby Square) Azenby (now Asenby) in Yorkshire. [1, 7, 370, 371]

B

BANSTEAD STREET 1883 (Surrey Lane) In an attempt to reduce the number of times Surrey was used in local names, the Surrey village of Banstead was chosen as an alternative. [1, 7]

BARFORTH LODGE, Barforth Road 1992 See Barforth Road [339]

BARFORTH ROAD 1868 Barforth in Durham [1 5 7]

BARNABY, 224 Ilderton Road (P) *Barnaby Rudge* by Charles Dickens. [23, 295]

BARSET ESTATE 1981-82 See Barset Road. [2]

BARSET ROAD 1877 (Salisbury Terrace) Probably in honour of Anthony Trollope's Barsetshire novels. *The Last Chronicle of Barset* was published in 1867. Trollope (1815-82) regarded it as his best novel. Salisbury was the main model for Barchester. [1, 4, 7, 23, 410]

BARSET WARD See Barset Road.

BARTON CLOSE, New James Street Estate 1978 Elizabeth Barton was a nun in the time of Henry VIII; she was known as the Holy Maid of Kent. She was beheaded at Tyburn on 20 April 1534 for predicting that the King would die suddenly if he persisted in his intention to divorce Catherine of Aragon and marry Anne Boleyn. Elizabeth Barton was said to be gifted with occult powers, and had a great following in her day. Even Sir Thomas More, the Lord Chancellor, believed in her prophesies. [2, 6, 88, 180, 340]

BASING COURT 1936 (Basing Place) Basing Manor House stood nearby. In writing about the Manor of Basing, W. H. Blanch stated: "This Manor gave name to a family of some note." [3, 8]

BASINGSTOKE HOUSE, Sumner Estate 1938 Basingstoke Canal. [1, 2, 12, 24]

BASSWOOD CLOSE, Linden Grove Estate 1980 Basswood is a variety of the lime tree family. [2, 168]

BATH CLOSE, Brimmington Estate 1978-80 Proximity to Asylum Road, formerly Bath Road. [2, 143]

BATTLE HOUSE, Friary Estate 1952 Benedictine community at Battle in East Sussex. [1, 5, 8, 14, 37]

BEDENHAM WAY, North Peckham Estate 1972 Bedenham in Hampshire. [2, 12, 15, 25]

BEECHDENE, Acorn Estate 1963 Beech tree. Dene means vale. [1, 2, 14, 19]

BEEHIVE, 122 Meeting House Lane (P) The beehive has long been a symbol of industry. [295]

BEESTON HOUSES, Consort Road 1834 Cuthbert Beeston, Master of the Worshipful Company of Girdlers in 1570. [11, 28]

BELFORT ROAD 1938 (Wellington Road) Belfort in France which suffered a siege of three months' duration during the Franco-Prussian War. Throughout the First World War Belfort was the right-hand pivot of the Allied line on the Western Front. [1, 8, 26]

BELLENDEN ROAD 1873 (Troy Villas, Victoria Terrace, Bellenden Terrace, Cedar Cottages, St. John's Terrace, Selwyn Terrace, Myrtle Villas, Oxford Terrace, Erith Villas, Devonshire Villas, Argyle Villas, Chapel Terrace, Ida Mount, Bellenden Villas, Leamington Villas, Meadow Terrace, Denmark Villas, Alpine Villas) Probably Lady Margaret Bellenden in Sir Walter Scott's novel *Old Mortality* (pub. 1816). The name was extended north along the present road, which originally consisted of numerous individually named groups and terraces, two of which were called Bellenden. The northern section, off Peckham High Street, was formerly Basing Road, and the manor house of Basing lay east of it. [1, 4, 7, 10, 23]

BELLENDEN SCHOOL, Reedham Street 1981 See Bellenden Road. [144]

BELLENDEN WARD See Bellenden Road.

BELLS GARDEN ROAD 1863 (Bell's Gardens' Road) Built on the site of nursery gardens belonging to Mr. Bell. [1, 3, 7, 10)

BELLS GARDENS ESTATE 1979-80 See Bells Garden Road. [2]

BELLWOOD ROAD, Waverley Park Estate 1887 Bellwood, in Midlothian, reminiscent of *Waverley* the first of the novels by Sir Walter Scott (pub. 1814). [1, 7, 23, 27]

BELVEDERE, 43 Linden Grove (P) 1851 Originally a kind of turret constructed in a high place so as to afford a "fine view", which is what the word means. [144, 295, 340]

BELVEDERE MEWS, Nunhead Grove 1989 Built near to "The Belvedere" public house. [170]

BIANCA ROAD 1879 Probably after Shakespeare's character in *The Taming of the Shrew.* [1, 7, 29]

BIBURY CLOSE, Gloucester Grove Estate 1974 Bibury in Gloucestershire. [5, 12, 400]

BIDWELL STREET 1868 Bidwell in Bedfordshire. [1, 5, 7]

BIRCH CLOSE, Atwell Estate c. 1964 Birch tree. [2]

BIRD-IN-BUSH ROAD 1873 (Hereford Place, Brunswick Terrace, Westbourne Terrace, Westbourne Cottages, Flora Cottages, Oxford Terrace, Montrose Cottages, Havelock Terrace, Radnor Terrace, Smyrren Terrace, Bournemouth Cottages, Cooper's Terrace) Revival of an early field name of which the derivation is unknown. [1, 8, 10]

BIRDLIP CLOSE, Gloucester Grove Estate 1974 Birdlip in Gloucestershire. [2, 5, 12, 400]

BISHOP WILFRED WOOD CLOSE, Moncrieff Street The Rt. Rev. Dr. Wilfred Wood became Bishop of Croydon in 1985. He officiated at the opening of the six family houses on 6 December, 1989. The houses were built for the African Refugee Housing Action Group. This was the first permanent housing scheme to house families who had to seek refuge in Britain from persecution and oppression in Africa and Third World countries. In recognition of the Bishop's record of support for housing initiatives, and for helping to meet the needs of refugees in particular, the houses were named after him. Bishop Wilfred Wood was Archdeacon of Southwark (1982-85). [193, 194, 195, 196]

BLACKPOOL ROAD 1938 (Russell Road 1872-1938) Blackpool in Lancashire. [1, 5, 8]

BLAKES ROAD 1878 (Elizabeth Terrace, Grove Terrace, George's Terrace, Gracefield Terrace, Mardling Terrace, Clifton Terrace, Sanders Terrace) Built on land owned by General Blake in the 1830s. [7, 232]

BLANCH CLOSE, Brimmington Estate 1981 Probably William Harnett Blanch. See *Who Was Who in Peckham.* [2, 17]

BLENDWORTH WAY, North Peckham Estate 1971 Blendworth in Hampshire. [2, 5, 12, 15]

BLENHEIM GROVE (Hollawell Terrace, Victoria Cottages, Dudley Cottages, Auckland Terrace) Dewhirst's 1842 map shows Marlborough House to the north of the High Street (where part of Oliver Goldsmith Estate is today). Opposite, on the south side of the High Street, Blenheim House is marked. Blenheim Grove is where it is today. In *Ye Parish of Camerwell* (1875) Blanch records: "Near the High Street, where Marlborough Road now stands, stood Marlborough House, a fine old mansion, supposed at one time to have been the residence of some portions of the Marlborough family. It has not been pulled down many years, and before its demolition it was used as a workhouse where the city paupers were farmed. The building contained a noble entrance-hall and a fine oak staircase, and frescoes adorned the walls and ceilings. Blenheim House, in the High Street, now occupied by Mr. Balls, is thought to have been a minor building attached to the mansion."

Blenheim Palace, seat of the Duke of Marlborough, near Woodstock in Oxfordshire, was conceived as a national monument and virtually as a royal palace. It was the gift of Queen Anne and Parliament to the 1st Duke in gratitude for his victory over the army of Louis XIV at the battle of Blenheim in 1704. [1, 3, 4, 8, 26, 143]

BOATHOUSE WALK 1892 (Maria Terrace, Angler's Terrace, Esther Place, Hayden Place, Globe Cottages, Amis Cottages, Bedford Place, Globe Place, Canal Bank). This path originally approached sheds for craft using the Grand Surrey Canal (completed in 1826; filled in during 1972). [1, 8, 10, 16]

BONAR ROAD 1894 Possibly hymn writer Horatius Bonar (1808-89). [1, 6, 8]

BOOTS, 20 Rye Lane (B) Jesse Boot (1850-1931), British entrepreneur and founder of a pharmacy chain. In 1863 Jesse Boot took over his father's small Nottingham shop trading in medicinal herbs. Recognising that the future lay with patent medicines, he concentrated on selling cheaply, advertising widely, and offering a wide range of medicines. In 1892 he began to manufacture drugs. Jesse Boot had more than 1,000 shops by his death. [227]

BORLAND ROAD 1863 (Marylebone Road, Arnolds Road, Alice Villas, Elsie Villas) John Borland served on Camberwell Vestry in 1870 and was a director of Peckham Pension Society. He lived at 184 High Street. [1, 3, 8, 10, 182]

BOURNEMOUTH CLOSE See Bournemouth Road.

BOURNEMOUTH ROAD 1866 Bournemouth in Dorset. [1, 5, 8]

BOWNESS HOUSE, Tustin Estate 1965 Bowness-on-Windermere in Cumbria. [2, 5]

B & Q DEPOT, Old Kent Road (B) Opened 31 January 1992. B & Q was formed in 1969 by Richard Block and David Quayle. [240, 241]

BRABOURN GROVE 1878 Henry Brabourne (alias Brabon), descended from John Brabourne keeper of the Hawks to Edward IV. The family was related by marriage to the Bowyer family. [2, 3, 8]

BRADFIELD CLUB, Commercial Way On 20 October 1891 a Men's Institute for the Parish of St. Luke, Camberwell, was founded at nos. 7 & 9 Commercial Road. It became known as St. Luke's Lads' Club and in December 1911 the Club was adopted by Bradfield College, Berkshire. Prince Philip visited Bradfield Club in 1952. He next visited in May 1985 when he opened the newly refitted building. [101, 102, 103]

BRAYARDS ROAD 1864 (Woodbine Cottages, Alice Terrace, Brockley Terrace, Chin Chu Cottages, Manvers Terrace, Victoria Terrace, Empress Terrace, Rock Terrace, Oakley Terrace, Lanvanor Terrace) An ancient arable field known as Brayard. [8, 125]

BRAYARDS ESTATE 1960 See Brayards Road. [2]

BREAMORE HOUSE, Friary Estate 1950 Austin Canons community at Breamore in Hampshire. [5, 14, 37, 361]

BRECKNOCK HOUSE, Sumner Estate 1938 Brecknock and Abergavenny Canal. [1, 2, 12, 30]

BREDINGHURST SCHOOL, Stuart Road Opened in 1948 in a building erected in 1874 for Camberwell Poor Law Union. The Manor of Bredinghurst or Bretinghurst at Peckham Rye was named after the Bretynghurst family. This Manor adjoined a Wood grubbed up in the middle of the 18th century. In an ancient Roll of the Barony of Maminot it was mentioned lying in Kent. There was a small bridge near which was a way leading to Bradinghurst; this was confirmed by an Inquisition taken in the reign of Richard II. [3, 353, 360]

BRIDGNORTH HOUSE, Friary Estate 1937 Franciscan community at Bridgnorth in Shropshire. [1, 5, 14, 37, 361]

BRIMMINGTON ESTATE 1978-82 Brimmington Road was one of the nineteenth century roads where the Brimmington Estate was built. It was named after Brimington (sic.) in Derbyshire. Three other adjacent streets had Derbyshire place names. [1, 2, 5, 21]

BRIMMINGTON PARK 1982 See Brimmington Estate. [345]

BROCKLEY FOOTPATH Perhaps from "Broca's Wood". [324]

BROCK STREET Late 1970s Charles Thomas Brock. See *Who Was Who in Peckham.* [17, 392]

BROCKWORTH CLOSE, Gloucester Grove Estate 1974 Brockworth in Gloucestershire. [5, 12, 400]

BROMYARD HOUSE, Ledbury Estate 1965 Bromyard in Hereford and Worcester. [2, 5]

BROOKSTONE COURT, Peckham Rye 1940 Businessmen Mr. Brook and Mr. Stone who were the first owners. [315]

BRUNSWICK WARD Celebrating the marriage of George IV to Caroline, daughter of the Duke of Brunswick. [1]

BRYANSTON HOUSE, Basing Court 1933 Built by Church Army Housing Association whose headquarters were in Bryanston Street, W1. [1, 171]

BUCHAN ROAD 1877 Possibly after Andrew Buchan (d. 1309?), Bishop of Caithness. [1, 6, 7]

BUDE HOUSE, Sumner Estate 1937 Bude Canal. [1, 2, 12, 31]

BUDLEIGH HOUSE, Lindley Estate 1964 (part of Sidmouth Grove Estate) Budleigh Salterton, Devon. [1, 2, 5]

BULLER CLOSE 1981 (part of Peckham Park Road) General Rt. Hon. Sir Redvers Henry Buller (1839-1908). His most famous, if controversial, command was in Natal during the Boer War of 1899-1900. [1, 10, 32, 400]

BULL YARD, Peckham High Street Next to the Red Bull public house.

BUNBURY HOUSE, Oliver Goldsmith Estate 1959 Amateur artist and caricaturist Henry William Bunbury (1750-1811) who was a friend of Oliver Goldsmith's. [2, 6, 14, 23]

BUN HOUSE, 96 Peckham High Street (P) 1898 On the site of a confectioner's. [321]

BURCHELL ROAD 1868 Probably after William John Burchell (1782?-1863), explorer and naturalist. (SHERWOOD) Probably laid out by Burchells, builders active in this area at the time. (FAIRFIELD) [1, 6, 7, 10]

BURGESS PARK Mrs. Jessie Burgess was first elected to the Metropolitan Borough of Camberwell in 1934. She was Camberwell's first woman Mayor (1945-47). In 1958, when she was 67, she was made an Honorary Freeman of the Borough of Camberwell. For 44 years she served on various committees of Camberwell Council and then Southwark Council. She died on 9 January 1981 in St. Francis Hospital, East Dulwich. [117, 118, 119]

BURGESS WARD See Burgess Park.

BURLINGTON COURT, Fenwick Road 1988 Property developers chose the name from the approved list of names suggested by Southwark Council. The list was compiled at random from the Outer London telephone directory. [201]

C

CADELEIGH ARMS, 43 Lyndhurst Grove (P) Probably Cadeleigh in Devon. [5]

CALEDONIAN HOUSE, 178 Queen's Road Origin not traced.

CAM COURT, Gloucester Grove Estate 1976 Cam in Gloucestershire. [2, 5, 12]

CAMDEN ESTATE Completed in 1976. Started by Camberwell Borough Council, it was designed in 1969.

Built on the sites of Camden Avenue, Camden Grove and Camden Street. Nearby was Camden Chapel which stood on the site now occupied by the block of flats in Peckham Road called Voltaire. Camden Chapel was built on a piece of ground in Camden Row Field leased from a Mr. Havill. The Chapel was opened on 10 September 1797 for the Countess of Huntingdon's Connexion. It was much enlarged in 1814 and was bombed in the Second World War. The Anglican parish of Camden was formed in 1844. [2, 3, 11, 12, 35, 61, 106, 107, 410]

CAMDEN SQUARE 1976 See Camden Estate. [2, 12]

CAMELOT SCHOOL, Bird-in-Bush Road Camelot School was built to replace Arthur Street School which was destroyed in World War II. Camelot was the name given in medieval romance to the seat of King Arthur, legendary king of Britain. [20, 26, 87]

CANAL BRIDGE, Old Kent Road Demolished 1992-93. Crossed Peckham branch of the Grand Surrey Canal. [20, 184]

CANAL GROVE The Grand Surrey Canal ran parallel with the north west side of this street. [2, 10]

CANAL HEAD 1913 The Peckham branch of the Grand Surrey Canal (completed in 1826) terminated here. [7, 16]

CANTERBURY ARMS, 871 Old Kent Road (P) On the road from London to Canterbury.

CANTIUM RETAIL PARK, Old Kent Road 1992 Cantium is Latin for Kent. [257, 258]

CAPUCHIN FRANCISCAN CHURCH OF OUR LADY OF SEVEN DOLOURS, Friary Road Opened on 4 October 1866 by Thomas Grant, Bishop of Southwark. Archbishop, later Cardinal, Manning preached the opening sermon.

Capuchins. A reform of the Franciscan order instituted by Matteo di Bessi of Urbino, who, being an Observantine Franciscan at Monte Falco, and having convinced himself that the *capuche* or cowl worn by St. Francis was different in shape from that worn by the friars of his own time, adopted a long-pointed cowl, according to what he conceived to be the original form.

Franciscans. This order takes its name from its founder St. Francis of Assisi, who died in 1226.

Dolour. Pain, grief, anger.

Dolours of the Blessed Virgin. St. John mentions that the Blessed Virgin, with other holy women and with St. John, stood at the foot of the cross when the other Apostles fled. The seven founders of the Servite order, in the thirteenth century, devoted themselves to special meditation on the Dolours of Mary, and from them the enumeration of the Seven Sorrows (i.e. at the prophesy of Simeon, in the flight to Egypt, at the three days' loss, at the carrying of the cross, at the crucifixion, at the descent from the cross, at the entombment) is said to have come. [210, 299, 300]

CARDEN ROAD 1868 Carden – a Cheshire parish. [1, 7, 25]

CARDIFF HOUSE, Friary Estate 1936 Franciscan community at Cardiff in South Glamorgan. [1, 5, 14, 37, 361]

CARDINE MEWS 1982 Elizabeth Cardine Naylor mentioned by L. S. Sherwood. Cardine is probably a misspelling of Caroline. Elizabeth Caroline Naylor was a resident of Peckham in the 19th century. See Naylor Road. [1, 180]

CARISBROOKE GARDENS, Rosemary Road 1962 Carisbrooke on the Isle of Wight. [5, 361]

CARLTON GROVE 1880 (Frances Terrace, Victoria Terrace, Lilbourne Cottages, Willow Cottages, Franks Cottages, Alice Cottages, Clyde Terrace) Possibly after politician Henry Boyle, Baron Carleton (d. 1725), owner of Carlton House, London. [1, 6, 7]

CARLTON TAVERN, 45 Culmore Road (P) c. 1855 Probably Baron Carleton. See Carlton Grove. [144]

CARNICOT HOUSE, Clifton Estate 1981 A misspelling of Carlingcott in Somerset. [2, 199, 200]

CAROLINE GARDENS, Asylum Road 1827-33 Caroline Sophie Secker. See *Who Was Who in Peckham.* [17, 144]

CASTLE HOUSE, 1-27 Sumner Road (B) Probably built in the 1930s but not named Castle House until 1988 when Newgate Press purchased the building. The reason for the name was that the firm's logo features a castle. [218]

CATOR STREET 1862 (James Street, John Street, Woodland Terrace, Nepaul Cottages, Wickwar Place) Probably P. Cator, a Governor of Dulwich College in 1858. [1, 3, 7]

CAULFIELD ROAD 1884 (Merton Terrace, Prince's Terrace, Horley Terrace and part of Lugard Road) Possibly James Caulfield (1764-1826), author and printseller. [1, 6, 7]

CAVERSHAM HOUSE, Friary Estate 1956 Caversham Court, a rectory of the Augustinian Canons, in Berkshire. [1, 169, 361]

CELESTIAL CHURCH OF CHRIST, Glengall Road Uses former St. Andrew's Church consecrated on 23 October 1865 by the Bishop of Winchester. The Celestial Church of Christ was founded in 1947 by the Reverend Pastor Prophet Founder Samuel Bilehou Joseph Oshoffa. The church's constitution states – The name of the Church came down from Heaven by divine revelation through Mr. Alexander Yanga, who was at that time undergoing spiritual healing at the residence of the Pastor Founder and who was held in trance for seven days. At the end of the seventh day, he asked for a piece of chalk and wrote the name of the Church on the wall thus: "EGLISE DU CHRISTIANISME CELESTE", meaning "Celestial Church of Christ". [3, 346, 347]

CERISE ROAD 1878 (Trench Road) Cerise was a daughter of Sir Claude Champion de Crespigny. She was born on 6 December 1875. In 1899 she married Capt. the Hon. Robert Francis Boyle (d. 1922). [1, 4, 7, 10, 47, 48]

CHADWICK ROAD 1877 (Albert Grove, Camden Terrace, Bodenberg Cottages, Albert Terrace, Raglan Cottages, Montague Cottages, Adelaide Terrace, Neptune Villas and Lime Cottages) William Chadwick (1797-1852), railway engineer and a wealthy freeholder. [1, 7, 10, 139, 180]

CHEAM STREET 1979 Cheam in the London Borough of Sutton. [5, 400]

CHELTENHAM ROAD 1938 (Hall Road) Cheltenham Villas, Hall Road. [7, 180]

CHEPSTOW WAY, Camden Estate 1975 Close to where Chepstow Terrace and Chepstow Hall used to be. [2, 178]

CHERRY TREE COURT, 1 Wood's Road 1974 The cherry tree from which Cherry Tree Court derived its name now stands outside the main entrance to Peckham Methodist Church. It was planted there by James Shirley when he was a tenant of 1 Harder's Road. (The cottage was demolished in 1972. At that time that part of Wood's Road was called Harder's Road.) Jim Shirley obtained the tree as a young sapling from an allotment in Crofton Park. He carried it to Peckham on a number 36 bus. This was in about 1960. The name Cherry Tree Court was suggested by Walter Finch who was a property steward of Peckham Methodist Church. [43]

CHESTERFIELD WAY 1978 Chesterfield in Derbyshire. [5, 400]

CHOUMERT GROVE 1877 (Albert Grove, Elizabeth Terrace, New Cottages and Hopewell Cottages) George Choumert. See *Who Was Who in Peckham*. [1, 7, 17]

CHOUMERT ROAD 1873 (Montpelier Road) See Choumert Grove. [1, 4, 7, 10]

CHOUMERT SQUARE See Choumert Grove.

CHRIST CHURCH, McDermott Road Erected in 1880. Named after the founder of the Christian Church. [286]

CHRIST CHURCH, Old Kent Road Consecrated on 1 July 1868. See above. [3]

CHURCH OF SAINT GEORGE, Newent Close Consecrated on 1 August 1982 by the Bishop of Southwark. St. George. [202]

CICELY ROAD 1878 (Rymill Road) Cicely, a daughter of Sir Claude Champion de Crespigny (b. 20 April 1847) of Champion Lodge, Camberwell. Cicely was born on 19 October 1874. On 19 March 1886 she married George Granville Lancaster (d. 1907), son of John Lancaster of Bilton Grange, Warwickshire. [1, 7, 10, 47, 48]

CITRON TERRACE, Linden Grove Estate 1980 Citron tree. [2, 168]

CLAIRE COURT, 98 Peckham Rye These flats were built by the Tilt Estate Company which was formed by Mr. H. J. Tilt in October 1934. When he retired his daughter, Mrs. Constance Harvey, became Governing

Director. She died on 21 May 1976 and left her Estate in trust to her daughter, Frances, and her three grandchildren, Claire, Tiffany and Dominic. This block of flats was named after Claire. Tiffany Court and Dominic Court, SE22, were named after the other two grandchildren. [83]

CLANFIELD WAY, North Peckham Estate 1971 Clanfield in Hampshire. [2, 5]

CLARKSON ARMS, 61 Carlton Grove (P) Origin not traced.

CLAUDE ROAD 1877 (Brinsmead Street, New Claude Road and Brighton Villas) Major Sir Claude Champion de Crespigny (b. 20 April 1847) who lived at Champion Lodge, Camberwell. He served in the Royal Navy (1860-65) and in the 60th Rifles (1866-70). He succeeded his father to the title as 4th Bart. in 1868. On 19 September 1872 he married Georgiana Louisa Margaret, second daughter of Robert McKerrell. They had nine children. Sir Claude was adjudged bankrupt in 1881. His estates were heavily mortgaged and his gross income from them had been reduced since 1868 from £8,000 a year to under £3,000. [1, 4, 8, 10, 47, 48]

CLAUDIA JONES YOUTH CLUB Used Bellenden Road School built in 1876. Claudia Jones (1915-64) was born in Port-of-Spain, Trinidad. She grew up in the urban poverty of Harlem. In her youth she was actively involved in organising in trade unions and became a member of the Communist Party of America. In 1948 she was arrested, tried and imprisoned for her political views and membership of the C.P.A. On release she was given the option of deportation to the West Indies or emigration. She chose the latter and Britain as her destination.

She arrived in Britain in 1955 and continued her political activity with the Communist Party of Great Britain and the Caribbean Labour Congress. She became an activist within the black community and helped to organise the carnivals set up in the wake of the 1958 Notting Hill riots.

During the same period she established, edited and published the Brixton based *West Indian Gazette.* Claudia Jones died in London and her grave is next to that of Karl Marx in Highgate Cemetery. [45, 46, 184]

CLAYTON ARMS, 1-5 Clayton Road (P) See Clayton Road.

CLAYTON ROAD 1880 (Elizabeth Place, Claro Cottages, Upper Clayton Road, Edward Villas, Cambridge Terrace, Ernest Terrace, Warwick Villas) Sir William Clayton (1762-1834), landowner of the site c. 1830. [1, 4, 10, 66, 232]

CLIFTON COURT, Studholme Street 1975 Built on the site of Clifton Congregational Church which was opened in 1859 and closed in 1972. [17, 21, 400]

CLIFTON CRESCENT 1881 (The Crescent, Clifton Grove) Clifton in Derbyshire. (One of a series of roads to the east of Asylum Road named after places in Derbyshire.) [5, 7, 21]

CLIFTON ESTATE 1967 Clifton Square was abolished to make way for the Clifton Estate. [2, 21]

CLIFTON WAY 1938 Clifton Way was called Clifton Road from 1867. Prior to that the houses were named Washington Villas, Commercial Place, Lansdowne Terrace and Olive Villas. In 1917 Clifton Villas and part of Carlton Place were incorporated into Clifton Road. [4, 7, 8, 21]

CLYDE HOUSE, Sumner Estate 1954 Forth and Clyde Canal. [1, 2, 12, 42]

COCKNEY'S, 610 Old Kent Road (P) In 1617 Minsheu wrote – A *Cockney* or *Cockny*, applied only to one borne within the sound of Bow-bell, that is within the City of London, which tearme came first out of this tale: That a Cittizens sonne riding with his father ... into the Country ... asked, when he heard a horse neigh, what the horse did his father answered, the horse doth neigh; riding farther he heard a cocke crow, and said doth the *cocke neigh* too? and therfore Cockney or Cocknie, by inuersion thus: *incock, q, incoctus* i. raw or vnripe in Country-mens affaires. [210]

COLEGROVE ROAD 1879 (Bangor Terrace and Langdale Road) Properly Colegrave. David Colegrave was a Camberwell Vestryman and Overseer of the Poor. He lived in Peckham Grove. (Blanch records numbers 54 and 64.) [1, 3, 7, 10]

COLESBOURNE COURT, Gloucester Grove Estate 1976 Colesbourne in Gloucestershire. [2, 5]

COLLEGE HALL, Burchell Road Part of Peckham Collegiate School which stood at the corner of Queen's Road and Burchell Road. In 1875 the School was run by the Rev. Thomas Ray, LL.D. [3]

COLLINSON HOUSE, Lindley Estate 1951 Peter Collinson. See *Who Was Who in Peckham.* [1, 2, 17]

COLLS ROAD 1874 Benjamin Colls who was a Camberwell Vestryman and a Guardian of the Poor. He was a successful builder active in South London in the 1860s. He lived at 246 Camberwell Road. [1, 3, 4, 7, 10, 78]

COLLYER PLACE 1881 (Collyer Cottages) Dr. William Bengo Collyer. See *Who Was Who in Peckham.* [1, 7, 10, 17]

COMET, Cantium Retail Park (B) Comet was named by the firm's founder, George Hollingbury. Unfortunately the exact origin of the name is not known. Comet began in 1933 in Hull as Comet Battery Services Limited. A store was opened in Hanover Park on 21 November 1987. This was closed when a larger store was opened in the Old Kent Road in 1992. [225, 226]

COMMERCIAL WAY 1936 (Commercial Road from 1871) The road bridged the Peckham branch of the Surrey Commercial Dock Company's Grand Surrey Canal which helped the establishment here of many small businesses. In the 19th century the street was called Commercial Road, the name replacing an earlier sequence of 35 names extending down the length of the street; two of these were Commercial Place and Commercial Terrace.

Commercial Wharf (later named Hope Wharf) was on the east bank of the canal just north of Globe Bridge. This was the only named wharf in 1842 on the system west of the Old Kent Road, except for the two terminal basins. In 1870 it was a timber wharf. [1, 7, 10, 62, 335]

CONSORT ESTATE 1978-81 See Consort Road. [2]

CONSORT PARK 1985 See Consort Road. [345]

CONSORT ROAD 1938 (Albert Road from 1879) Albert, Prince Consort (1819-61), husband of Queen Victoria. The name was changed because there were many other "Albert" street names. The road was built along the line of an old lane called Cow Walk. [1, 8, 10, 26, 190]

CONSORT WARD See Consort Road.

CONSTANCE COURT, 47 Blenheim Grove 1983 Built by Tilt Estate Company and named after the daughter of the founder of Tilt, Mrs. Constance Harvey. She took over the company from her father, Mr. H. J. Tilt. Constance Harvey died on 21 May 1976. [63, 83]

CO-OPERATIVE HOUSE, Rye Lane (B) The Royal Arsenal Co-operative Society (formed in 1868) opened a store at 259-267 Rye Lane in 1913. This was remodelled and opened as Co-operative House on 12 October 1932. The store closed in 1980. [220]

COPELAND ROAD 1868 (Cow Lane, Copeland Terrace, Woodbine Terrace, Caroline Terrace, John's Terrace and Royal Terrace) Chief Justice John Copeland. He was an active member of Hanover Chapel during the time of Dr. John Milner. He contributed to the building fund. He died at Peckham on 21 or 22 August 1761 aged 87. [1, 3, 7, 10, 17, 67, 254, 330, 331, 332]

COPLESTON CENTRE, Copleston Road See Copleston Road. The Copleston Centre was opened in 1979 in St. Saviour's Church. [79]

COPLESTON MEWS 1990 See Copleston Road. [184]

COPLESTON ROAD 1873 (Rose Bank, Clyde Villas, Elizabeth Villas, Claremont Villas, Bulmer Villas, Herbert Villas, Dynevon Villas, Swiss Villas, Clyde Terrace, Brooklyn Villas, Cleveland Villas, Clara Villas and Arthur Terrace; from 1903 Placquett Road and Ardley Terrace became part of Copleston Road) Edward Copleston (1776-1849), Bishop of Llandaff. [1, 6, 7, 10]

COPNER WAY, North Peckham Estate 1971 Copner, a district of Portsmouth in Hampshire. [2, 5]

CORINTH HOUSE, Sumner Estate 1938 Corinth Canal, a tidal waterway across the Isthmus of Corinth in Greece, joining the Gulf of Corinth in the north west with the Saronic Gulf in the south east. It was opened in 1893. [1, 2, 64]

COSSALL ESTATE 1977-81 See Cossall Walk. Cossall Street (1868) was off Burchell Road and was one of a number of Victorian streets demolished to make way for Cossall Estate. [2, 7, 21]

COSSALL PARK See Cossall Walk. The park was created in 1977. [43]

COSSALL WALK 1977 Cossall in Nottinghamshire. [1, 2, 5]

COSTA STREET 1874 (South Street, Garibaldi Cottages, St. James's Terrace, Regent's Place, Rose Cottages and Howard Terrace) Probably Sir Michael Costa (1810-84), a conductor and musical composer born in Naples, Italy. He conducted at Crystal Palace which was particularly famous for the performances of music written by George Frederick Handel. The first "Great Handel Festival" was held in 1857. There were over 2,000 singers and 386 instrumentalists in the central transept of the Palace, conducted by Michael Costa. The Great Handel Festival was such a success that it was repeated in 1859 to commemorate the centenary of the composer's death. After that, similar events were held every three years. Until 1880 they were conducted by Michael Costa. [1, 6, 7, 65]

COTTAGE WALK, Camden Estate 1976 Cottage Grove was demolished when the Camden Estate was built. [2, 7, 400]

CRABTREE WALK, Camden Estate 1976 Close to where Crab Tree Shot Road used to be. Crab Tree Shot was a field name in the lands owned by the Trevors, by Martha Hill and later by the Shards. [2, 7, 410]

CRANE HOUSE, Pelican Estate 1964 Water-fowl. [1, 2]

CREDENHILL HOUSE, Ledbury Estate 1967 Credenhill in Hereford and Worcester. [2, 5]

CREED HOUSE, Nunhead Estate 1956 George Creed (1807-82) omnibus proprietor in the parish of Camberwell. [1, 2, 3, 340]

CREWYS ROAD 1877 Believed to be misspelt. Cruwys-Morchard in Devon. [1, 5, 7]

CRINAN HOUSE, Sumner Estate 1938 Crinan Canal in Scotland. [1, 2, 42]

CROMFORD HOUSE, Sumner Estate 1937 Cromford Canal in Derbyshire. [1, 2, 42]

CROWN, 119 Peckham High Street (P) Blanch (1875) wrote:- "John Barleycorn* is proverbially loyal, and therefore 'The Crown' (High Street, Peckham) is a favourite sign." (*The personification of alcoholic drink.) [3]

CROWN MANSIONS, Peckham High Street Crown Theatre was opened in 1898 on the corner of Marmont Road and the High Street (where the bingo hall is today). It was later known as the Peckham Hippodrome. [16, 35]

CULMORE ROAD 1872 (Carlton Road, Culmore Terrace, Lincoln Terrace, Falcon Terrace, Shaftesbury Villas) Possibly Culmore in Ireland. [1, 7]

CURLEW HOUSE, Pelican Estate 1957 Water-fowl. [1, 2]

D

DANBY STREET 1873 (Wilton Terrace, Love Villas, Norbury Villas, Tudor Villas, Woodbine Villas, Macduff Terrace, Danby Villas, Victoria Villas, Myrtle Villas, Box Villas, Ashbourne Villas, St. Ivians Villas, Laurel Villas, Niton Villas, Gloucester Villas, Danby Terrace, The Firs, Crystal Villas, Danby Cottages) Danby Villas, Danby Terrace and Danby Cottages. Danby may have been the builder of these three. [1, 7, 10]

DANIEL GARDENS 1938 (Daniel Street) Probably Rev. G. W. Daniel, Chaplain to Dulwich College. [1, 8, 80]

DANIELS ROAD 1863 Henry Daniel (1805-67) was a monumental mason and was the first to establish a mason's yard at Nunhead. His workshops were opposite the cemetery's main gates in Linden Grove. Henry Daniel served on Camberwell Vestry in the 1860s. He was buried in his family vault. Nunhead Cemetery closed in 1969 and Henry Daniel's old house, a landmark for over a century, and his workshops were demolished. [7, 10, 81, 145, 180]

DANUBE COURT, Daniel Gardens 1971 River Danube. [26, 361]

DAVEY STREET 1863 Probably Peter Davey, tenant of land nearby c. 1830. He lived at Champion Hill. [1, 7, 60]

DAYTON GROVE 1880 Origin not traced. [7]

DEERHURST HOUSE, Friary Estate 1956 A Benedictine house at Deerhurst in Gloucestershire. [1, 14, 37, 361]

DE LAUNE CYCLING CLUB, 93 Choumert Road 1971 Mr. Chapman Delaune Faunce-De Laune (d. 1893). High Sheriff of Kent in 1886, landowner and magistrate. He lived at Sharsted Court, Sittingbourne. [355, 356]

DENMAN ARMS, 86 Denman Road (P) See Denman Road. [3]

DENMAN ROAD 1858 (Ash Villas, Abbey Cottages, Grove Villas, Cleveland Villas, Oakfield Terrace, Oak Villas, Magdala Terrace, Georgie Cottages, Rose Cottages, Myrtle Cottages and Colaba Villas) Thomas, Baron Denman (1779-1854) who was made Attorney General in 1830. This is one of a group of names taken from the legal profession. [1, 3, 6, 7, 10]

DENMEAD WAY, North Peckham Estate 1971 Denmead in Hampshire. [2, 5]

DENSTONE HOUSE, Friary Estate 1952 Denstone in Staffordshire. Denstone College was founded by Nathaniel Woodard in 1873. The Woodard School is a religious foundation. [1, 5, 68]

DEVONSHIRE GROVE 1900 County of Devon or the Earls of Devon. [1, 7]

DEVON STREET 1938 (Devonshire Street) County of Devon or the Earls of Devon. [1, 8, 20]

DEWAR STREET 1876 Sir James Dewar (1842-1923), British chemist and physicist who invented the vacuum flask. [1, 7, 10, 26]

DIAMOND STREET 1890 (Shakespeare Terrace, Diamond Cottages, Rosemary Cottages) Built by a plumber whose diamond brought him the means to build the street. [1, 3, 7, 10, 143]

DOWNEND COURT, Gloucester Grove Estate 1976 Downend in Avon. [2, 5]

DROITWICH HOUSE, Sumner Estate 1938 Droitwich Canal. [1, 2, 69]

DROVERS, 720/722 Old Kent Road (P) Formerly the Kentish Drovers which appears to be first mentioned on Cary's map of 1830. It is assumed that the name derived from the fact that in the days of "animals on the hoof", on the way to Smithfield Market in London, the Old Kent Road was a much frequented drove road. [3, 293, 341]

DROVERS PLACE 1987 Not far from Drovers pub (see above) where a mural depicts rural Peckham. [184, 203, 400]

DUKE OF SUSSEX, 77 Friary Road (P) 1906 The Duke of Sussex had links with Peckham. He attended the opening of Hanover Chapel on 17 June 1817. He was a son of King George III. [3, 410]

DUNDAS ROAD 1871 Sir Thomas Dundas, art collector. [1, 7, 10, 80]

DUNSTALL HOUSE, Oliver Goldsmith Estate 1955 John Dunstall played Jarvis in *The Good Natur'd Man* by Oliver Goldsmith. [1, 2, 93]

DURSLEY COURT, Gloucester Grove Estate 1976 Dursley in Gloucestershire. [2, 5]

DYMOCK COURT, Gloucester Grove Estate 1975 Dymock in Gloucestershire. [2, 5]

E

EAGLE WHARF, Peckham Hill Street Eagle Saw Mill was situated on the east side of the Peckham branch of the Grand Surrey Canal where Eagle Wharf is today. "The Eagle" public house was in nearby Bells Garden Road. A Christian and heraldic symbol, the eagle has been used as an inn sign since the 15th century. [17, 21, 62, 295]

EAST DULWICH BAPTIST CHURCH, Amott Road Opened on 9 August 1958. Dulwich may come from two Old English words, Dill, a white flower, and wihs, meaning a damp meadow. Dulwich was "the meadow where dill grows". Baptists trace their origins in modern times to the action of John Smyth, a Separatist exile in Amsterdam who, in 1609, reinstituted the baptism of conscious believers as the basis of the fellowship of a gathered Church. [207, 284, 285]

EAST DULWICH ROAD ESTATE 1954 See East Dulwich Baptist Church. [2]

EAST SURREY GROVE 1862 (Swan Terrace, Caroline's Terrace, Mary's Terrace, James Grove) Peckham was in Surrey until the London County Council came into being in 1889. As many London streets used the name Surrey, East may have been added to distinguish it from others. Sherwood suggested that it probably commemorated the battle honours of the East Surrey Regiment but that name was not used until 1881. Villiers' Regiment of Marines (31st Foot in 1751) and 2nd Battalion of the 31st Foot in 1756 (70th Foot in 1758) became the 1st and 2nd Battalions of the East Surrey Regiment in 1881. [1, 7, 362, 363]

EATON WALK, Camden Estate 1975 Close to where Eaton Place used to be. [2, 155]

EBLEY CLOSE, Gloucester Grove Estate 1974 Ebley in Gloucestershire. [5, 400]

EDINBURGH CASTLE, 57 Nunhead Lane (P) 1935 The castle is famous well beyond Scotland because of its annual military tattoo. [295, 296, 340]

EDNAM HOUSE, Friary Estate 1957 A medieval religious house at Ednam in Scotland. [175, 361]

EDWIN HOUSE, Oliver Goldsmith Estate 1959 *The Hermit, or Edwin and Angelina,* a ballad by Oliver Goldsmith written in 1764, and included in *The Vicar of Wakefield.* Angelina, benighted in the wilderness, and sorrowing for her lost Edwin, whom she believes dead, is welcomed to the Hermit's cell and in answer to his question reveals the cause of her sorrow. The Hermit then acknowledges himself to be Edwin. [2, 23]

EGLINGTON COURT, East Dulwich Road Estate 1954 Rev. Arthur Eglington, Vicar of St. John's, Goose Green, 1901-09. [1, 2, 82, 398]

ELCOT AVENUE 1878 (Stanley Villas) Probably after Elcot Park, near Newbury in Berkshire, laid out by Sir William Paxton in 1848. [1, 7, 75]

ELFRIDA RATHBONE SCHOOL, Reddins Road Elfrida Rathbone (1871-1940) was born in Liverpool into a well-to-do family well-known for its philanthropic activities and prominent in local affairs.

She was one of eleven children. In 1916 Elfrida Rathbone became a teacher in a special kindergarten for mentally handicapped children in the King's Cross area of London. Three years later she established an Occupation Centre for "ineducable" children who were excluded from schools. The work there proved that these outcast children could be taught and trained successfully while remaining in the community. This venture proved so successful that in 1922 it was taken over and run by a well established charity, The Central Association for Mental Health.

Elfrida Rathbone recruited people to sit on the Care Committees of Islington's Special Schools for "mentally defective" children so that their needs could be better met. Consequently children who had previously been excluded were able to enjoy school, holidays, convalescence, outings and parties.

As the children whom Elfrida Rathbone had taught in the kindergarten reached school leaving age, the need for an After Care provision became a priority. In 1923 a Girls Club was formed followed by a Married Girls class with a creche. In 1930 a befriending scheme was set up for those rejected mentally defective children confined in a Public Assistance home and other types of institutions.

Elfrida Rathbone fought for the rights and interests of a group of people rejected, stigmatised and punished by society because of handicaps they suffered through no fault of their own. [76]

ELIM HOUSE, 86 Bellenden Road Formerly Peckham Seventh Day Adventist Church, Elim House was opened in 1987 as the base of the Black Elderly Group Southwark. The name Elim House was decided upon following a competition among the users of the centre to give the new centre a name. Elim is a biblical name meaning place of rest and refreshment. [123, 256]

ELKSTONE COURT, Gloucester Grove Estate 1976 Elkstone in Gloucestershire. [2, 5]

ELLAND ROAD 1869 (Elland Street) Elland in West Yorkshire. In 1869 Thomas Drake applied to the Metropolitan Board of Works to register two streets – Elland Road and Siddall Street. Siddal (sic.) is in West Yorkshire. [1, 5, 7, 204, 283]

ELLERY STREET 1879 (George Street) Possibly in honour of Robert Lewis John Ellery (1827-1908), Government astronomer of Victoria, Australia. He was born at Cranleigh in Surrey and visited England in 1875 when he attended a dinner to celebrate the bi-centenary of the foundation of the Royal Observatory. [1, 7, 205, 206]

ELLESMERE HOUSE, Sumner Estate 1951 Ellesmere and Chester Canal. [1, 2, 77]

ELM GROVE 1889 (Elm Villas, Barton Terrace, Washington Place, Elm Cottages, Priory Villas, The Priory) Elm Villas and Elm Cottages. [1, 4, 7]

ELMHURST VILLAS, Peckham Rye Close to the site of a house called Elmhurst. [154]

ELY HOUSE, Friary Estate 1950 Benedictine community at Ely in Cambridgeshire. [1, 5, 14, 37, 308, 361]

EMANUEL MIRACLE TEMPLE OF BETHANY FELLOWSHIP OF GREAT BRITAIN, 36-38 Gautrey Road In 1991 this church moved into the former Nunhead Baptist Church, opened in 1889. Emanuel means "God with us" and the church felt that God guided them over the purchase of the premises. The congregation was previously based in Wandsworth where miracles are said to have occurred. [383, 384]

ETHNARD ROAD 1888 (Moor Terrace, Union Cottages and part of Downes Street). Not traced. Sherwood wrote: "This could have been misread for Edward Road. Try writing Edward six times very carelessly and see the result!" More likely to be Ethnam in Kent misspelt. [1, 4, 7, 283]

EVAN COOK LTD., 134 Queen's Road (B) Evan Cook. See *Who Was Who in Peckham.* [17]

EVELINA ROAD 1869 (Argyle Terrace, Craven Terrace, Oxford Terrace, East Terrace, West Terrace and parts of Cemetery Road and Lausanne Road) Probably *Evelina,* a novel by Frances Burney (1752-1840) whose family lived over the border in Deptford. [1, 7, 23]

EVERTHORPE ROAD 1902 (Placquett Terrace and Normanton Terrace) Probably the hamlet of Everthorpe in Humberside. [2, 5, 7]

EXETER HOUSE, Friary Estate 1936 Franciscan community at Exeter in Devon. [1, 5, 14, 37, 308, 361]

EXETER ROAD, Camden Estate 1976 Exeter Place was demolished when the Camden Estate was built. [2, 7, 400]

F

FAITH CHAPEL, Bellenden Road Opened in 1885 as a United Methodist Free Church. Bought by Hanover Chapel in 1922. After Hanover United Reformed Church moved to St. Saviour's Church, Copleston Road, in 1979 the building was bought by a congregation affiliated to the Pentecostal Assemblies of the World and renamed Faith Chapel. This name was chosen because the congregation had faith that they would manage to raise the money to buy the church. They had only £2,000 and the price was over £50,000. Hanover URC accepted £30,000 and the congregation succeeded in raising this amount. Their faith was justified so Faith Chapel became the new name and it opened in 1979. [67, 312, 313]

FALCON HOUSE, Pelican Estate 1964 Falcon, a bird of prey. [1, 2]

FARNBOROUGH WAY, North Peckham Estate 1971 Farnborough in Hampshire. [2, 5]

FENHAM ROAD 1866 Fenham in Northumberland. [1, 4, 5, 7]

FENWICK GROVE 1889 (Gledhill Road) Possibly Fenwick in South Yorkshire. [1, 5, 7]

FENWICK ROAD 1867 See Fenwick Grove. [1, 7]

FERNHOLME ROAD 1894 Fernholme: Holm = holly or island. [7, 350]

FILTON COURT, Gloucester Grove Estate 1977 Filton in Avon, formerly Gloucestershire. [2, 5, 9]

FINCHDEAN WAY, North Peckham Estate 1971 Finchdean in Hampshire. [2, 5]

FIRBANK ROAD 1877 Built on land which belonged to a Mr. Firbank in the 1870s. [1, 7, 10]

FLAMBOROUGH HOUSE, Oliver Goldsmith Estate 1956 Solomon Flamborough in *The Vicar of Wakefield* by Oliver Goldsmith. [2, 90]

FORESTER ROAD 1868 (The Avenue) Probably Sir Philip Forester in *My Aunt Margaret's Mirror* by Sir Walter Scott. [1, 7, 90]

FRANCIS BACON LODGE, Waghorn Street English statesman, essayist and philosopher Francis Bacon (1561-1626). The Rosicrucians, members of a mystical brotherhood, meet in this former St. Andrew's Mission Church built in 1902. This non-sectarian philosophic and scientific fraternity is known as the Ancient Mystical Order Rosae Crucis (AMORC). In the words of Bacon, its aim is "To glorify God and benefit man's estate". [26, 398]

FRASER LODGE, 42-44 Stuart Road Origin not traced.

FREDA CORBET CLOSE 1983 Freda Künzlen Corbet (1900-) was educated at Wimbledon County School and University College London. She was called to the Bar, Inner Temple, in 1932. She was M.P. for N.W. Camberwell (1945-50) and the Peckham division of Camberwell (1950-74). [91, 95, 400]

FREE TRADER, 35 Green Hundred Road (P) The free trade doctrine is that international trade should be free of all restrictions, such as import duties or quotas. In the 1840s its main advocates were John Bright, M.P. for Manchester, and Richard Cobden, M.P. for Stockport. The Liberal Party adopted it as official policy, and it became national policy between 1860 and 1932. [295]

FRENSHAM STREET 1892 (Surrey Terrace and Canal Cottages) Frensham in Surrey. (Name chosen to reduce the number of street names beginning with Surrey.) [1, 5, 7]

FRIARY ESTATE See Friary Road

FRIARY ROAD 1935 (Lower Park Road) Renamed in honour of the Franciscan Church and Monastery in this road. [1, 8, 299]

FRIARY WARD See Capuchin Franciscan Church of our Lady of Seven Dolours.

FROME HOUSE, Rye Hill Estate 1938 River Frome. [2, 92]

FURLEY HOUSE, Friary Estate 1947 See Furley Road. [8]

FURLEY ROAD 1936 (Furley Street 1876 and Nelson Square) Furley in Devon. [1, 5, 7, 8, 21]

G

GALATEA SQUARE 1979 Close to where Galatea Road was built in 1868. Galatea was a sea nymph in Greek mythology. In John Gay's libretto to Handel's "Acis and Galatea" (1732) the contrast of the dainty sea nymph and the clumsy giant is pleasantly brought out by the music. [1, 7, 21, 94, 180]

GANNET HOUSE, Pelican Estate 1957 Gannet (seabird). [1, 2, 26]

GARDEN COURT, Camden Estate 1975 Garden Cottages were nearby in the 19th century. [2, 7]

GARNIES CLOSE, North Peckham Estate 1951-58 Close to where Garnies Street used to be. Edward Street became Garnies Street in 1882. Believed to have been named after Martin Garnar, Camberwell Vestryman in 1875. [1, 2, 7, 96]

GATEFIELD COURT, East Dulwich Road Estate 1954 The plot of land on which St. John's Church stands was called Gatefield or Catfield. [1, 2]

GAUTREY ROAD 1937 (Edith Road) Thomas Gautrey. See *Who Was Who in Peckham.* [1, 8, 10, 17]

GELDART ROAD 1883 Edmund Martin Geldart (1844-1885) Unitarian Minister. In 1877 he became minister of the Free Christian Church in Croydon. [1, 7, 104, 105]

GEORGE, 231 St. George's Way (P) St. George. [298]

GERVASE STREET 1879 (George Street, Elizabeth Cottages, Charles Terrace) Possibly Gervase of Canterbury (c. 1145-1210), English chronicler, monk of Christ Church, Canterbury. Gervase Street is close to Christ Church and the Old Kent Road. [1, 7, 26]

GIBBON ROAD 1869 (Cemetery Road, Lausanne Road (part), Alexandra Terrace, Oswald Terrace, Fairlight Terrace, St. John's Terrace, St. James Terrace, Linden Terrace) Charles Gibbon. See *Who Was Who in Peckham.* [1, 7, 10, 17]

GIRDLERS COTTAGES, Choumert Road 1851 (Palyn's Almshouses) Built by The Worshipful Company of Girdlers. [3, 28, 144]

GISBURN HOUSE, Friary Estate 1950 Austin Canons community at Gisburn in Lancashire. [1, 5, 14, 37 361]

GLENGALL ARMS, 41 Glengall Road (P) See Glengall Road.

GLENGALL ROAD 1880 (Glengall Grove, Derwent Road, Alexander Terrace, Derwent Terrace) The Countess of Glengall owned land in Peckham. Lady Glengall, who married into the Irish peerage in 1834, was formerly Miss Margaret Lauretta Mellish, daughter and co-heir of William Mellish, a multi-millionaire and government contractor of Woodford, Essex. [1, 7, 10]

GLENGALL TAVERN, 1 Bird-in-Bush Road (P) Close to Glengall Road.

GLENGALL TERRACE See Glengall Road.

GLOBE, 58 Peckham Hill Street (P) A name now associated with Shakespeare because of the Globe Theatre, where his plays were performed during his lifetime. The Globe has always been a popular pub sign, and there are at least twenty pubs of this name in London. [295, 296]

GLOUCESTER GROVE ESTATE 1972-78 See Gloucester School Gloucester Road was demolished to make way for the estate. [2, 20]

GLOUCESTER SCHOOL, Daniel Gardens 1875 Robert Earl of Gloucester who was Lord of the Peckham Manor. [16, 124, 125, 376]

GLOVER HOUSE, Nunhead Estate 1951 John Glover was a coachmaster in the parish of Camberwell in the 19th century. [1, 2, 3]

GODMAN ROAD 1878 (Donald Road) General Richard Temple Godman, Lieut.-Col. commanded 5th dragoon guards. He married Eliza Mary de Crespigny on 29 July 1871. She was a daughter of Sir William de Crespigny (b. June 1818). [1, 2, 10, 47]

GOLDEN ANCHOR, 16 Evelina Road (P) An heraldic reference to the arms of the Lord High Admiral. [295]

GOLDEN LION, 133 Sumner Road (P) A popular sign, referring heraldically to Henry I, or to the dukes of Northumberland, the Percys. [295]

GOLDSMITH ROAD 1872 (Back Walk, Park Lane, Daniel's Terrace, Francis Place, Park Terrace) Oliver Goldsmith. See *Who Was Who in Peckham.* [1, 7, 10, 17]

GOODWIN HOUSE, Nunhead Estate 1956 Mr. Goodwin was a local coachmaster in the 19th century. [1, 2, 3]

GORDON ROAD 1875 (Stanley Villas, Hawthorn Villas, Hermon Cottages, The Terrace, Bordeaux Cottages, Nichol's Terrace, Gordon Cottages, Gordon Terrace North, Gordon Terrace, Magdala Terrace, Albion Terrace, India Terrace, Ann's Cottages, Wellington Terrace) General Charles George Gordon (1833-85), British soldier, the hero of Khartoum, born at Woolwich. [1, 4, 6, 10, 26]

GOSPORT WAY, North Peckham Estate 1971 Gosport in Hampshire. [2, 5]

GOWLETT ARMS, 62 Gowlett Road (P) See Gowlett Road.

GOWLETT ROAD 1879 (Gowlett Terrace) Believed to be the name of the builder. [1, 7]

GRANGE COURT, 101 Talfourd Road 1963 A private estate, named by the owners for personal reasons. [1]

GRANTHAM HOUSE, Friary Estate 1939 Franciscan religious house at Grantham in Lincolnshire. [1, 5, 14, 37, 308, 361]

GRANVILLE SQUARE 1987 Originally "Pepys Square" was chosen but this was turned down as there is a Pepys Road in SE14. A selection of names was chosen at random by the developers, Balfour Beatty Homes, and Granville Square was accepted by the London Borough of Southwark. [208, 209]

GRASMERE POINT, Tustin Estate 1965 Grasmere in Cumbria, [2, 5]

GRATELEY WAY, North Peckham Estate 1971 Grateley in Hampshire. [2, 5]

GREEN HUNDRED ROAD 1877 Revival of an early place name. The Green Hundred was a plot of land held by the Gardyner family. [1, 8, 10]

GREYHOUND, 109 Peckham High Street (P) Blanch (1875) refers to an unknown man who died at the Greyhound in 1747. The present building is not the original one. The sign, which dates from Tudor kings, appeared on the coats of arms of both Henry VII and VIII. [3, 297]

GREYSTOKE HOUSE, Friary Estate 1954 Greystoke in Cumbria. The Collegiate Church of Greystoke has deep roots in the past for it is interesting to note that the College of Priests founded 600 years ago was restarted again in 1957. [1, 70, 361]

GRIMWADE CRESCENT 1877 Local landowner and builder of that street. [1, 7, 10]

GROVE NURSERY SCHOOL, Newent Close 1976 Built to serve the Gloucester Grove and North Peckham Estates. [375]

GROVE VALE ESTATE 1903 Grove Vale – from its natural contrast to Grove Hill. [1, 16]

GRUMMANT ROAD 1866 John Grummant was a Camberwell Vestryman and was an owner of a large amount of property in the parish of Camberwell. He lived at 1 Lawn Houses, Peckham Road. [1, 3, 7]

HALFORDS, Unit 2B Cantium Retail Park, Old Kent Road (B) Opened 4 April 1992. Halfords was founded in 1892 by Frederick William Rushbrooke, a wholesale ironmonger. The name comes from the address of a warehouse that opened in 1902 in Halford Street, Leicester. The company officially adopted the name Halfords in 1965. [276, 277]

HANOVER PARK pre 1842 Named after Hanover Chapel (the remains of which can still be seen at the corner of Rye Lane and the High Street) attended by the Dukes of Kent and Sussex. The close union of members of the Royal House of Hanover with Dr. William Bengo Collyer led to the Meeting House receiving the name of Hanover Chapel. [1, 4, 7, 10, 17, 67, 143]

HARDCASTLE HOUSE, Oliver Goldsmith Estate 1954 Mr. Hardcastle, a country squire, in *She Stoops to Conquer* by Oliver Goldsmith. [1, 2, 90]

HARDER'S ROAD 1893 (Harders Place, Maud Villas, Gunnersbury Villas, Linden Villas, Cambrian Terrace, Mortlock Terrace, Lowless Terrace, Lansdowne Villas) Mr. Harder was a landowner in Peckham. [1, 4, 7, 10]

HARDER'S ROAD MEWS See Harder's Road.

HARLESCOTT ROAD 1886 Harlescott in Shropshire. [5, 7]

HARRY LAMBORN HOUSE, 9 Gervase Street 1984 Harry Lamborn. See *Who Was Who in Peckham.* [17, 97, 98, 99]

HASTINGS CLOSE, Bells Gardens Estate 1979 George Hastings in *She Stoops to Conquer* by Oliver Goldsmith. [2, 23, 93, 400]

HATCHAM ROAD 1876 (Samuel Place, Albert Place, Albion Place, Child's Place) The Saxon manor of Hatcham was called Hacchesham, meaning the home of Hacca. Its ownership is first recorded in 1086, and last in the mid-18th century. A map of 1744 shows Hatcham House, moated and with extensive grounds. [7, 10, 369]

HATHORNE CLOSE 1961 Hathorne, a plot of land in Dulwich. [1, 80, 172]

HAVANT WAY, North Peckham Estate 1972 Havant in Hampshire. [2, 5]

HAVELOCK ARMS, 38 Meeting House Lane (P) Sir Henry Havelock (1795-1857), British soldier who achieved the relief of Lucknow. [26, 295]

HAWKSLADE ROAD 1894 Hawk<u>slade</u>: Slade = valley or dell. [7, 350]

HAYMERLE HOUSE, Friary Estate 1942 See Haymerle Road. [8]

HAYMERLE ROAD 1879 (Belgrave Terrace, Argyle Terrace, Belgrave Place, Charterhouse Street) Baron Heinrich von Haymerle (1828-80). Austro-Hungarian minister at the Congress of Berlin in 1878. He was Prime Minister and Foreign Minister of the dual monarchy 1879-80. [1, 4, 7, 10, 100]

HAZEL CLOSE, Atwell Estate 1963 Hazel tree. [2, 26]

HEATON, 249 Rye Lane (P) Adjacent to Heaton Road.

HEATON ROAD 1868 (Heaton Villas) Isaac Heaton. See *Who Was Who in Peckham.* Isaac Heaton was brother-in-law of Sir Claude Champion de Crespigny. [1, 7, 10, 17, 47, 180]

HEATON ROAD CHURCH, Heaton Road Opened on 21 September 1873. See Heaton Road. [3]

HELENA DAY NURSERY, Camden Square Councillor Mrs. Helena Day who served on Camberwell and Southwark Councils from 1949 to 1977. She was elected leader of Southwark Council's Tory opposition in 1974. She died in 1977 aged 85. [223, 233, 234]

HENLEY COURT, Peckham Rye 1990 Selected by the developers of the property "because they felt it to be a nice name". It sounded attractive because of its association with Henley Regatta. [235, 404]

HENSLOW HOUSE, Lindley Estate 1948 Botanist John Stevens Henslow (1796-1861). [1, 2, 6]

HEREFORD RETREAT, Bird-in-Bush Road Revival of name of row of 19th century houses behind St. Andrew's Church. Origin of name not traced. [7, 20]

HERON HOUSE, Pelican Estate 1957 Heron. All the blocks on this estate are named after birds. [1, 2, 26]

HEVERSHAM HOUSE, Tustin Estate 1965 Heversham in Cumbria. [2, 5]

HICHISSON ROAD 1891 (Paddington Road, Oxford Villas, Kingsdown Villas, Cambridge Villas, Marlborough Villas) Joseph Geldart Hichisson was active in Camberwell's local government. He was a Vestryman in the 1890s and later served on Camberwell Borough Council as an Alderman. [1, 7, 10]

HIGHSHORE ROAD 1938 (Hanover Street) See Highshore School. [8]

HIGHSHORE SCHOOL, Bellenden Road Opened on 30 January 1970. In 1955 water deep down showed where an old stream flowed to the Peckham branch of the Grand Surrey Canal. During the building of the present school, this watercourse was again uncovered. The "adventure hill" marks the point of the High Shore above the watercourse. It is probable that in days gone by this zone was referred to as the Highshore. An 18th century map shows a stream from the hills beyond passing the area where the school now stands on its way to the Thames. [366, 380]

HILLBECK CLOSE 1969 Hillbeck in Cumbria. [2, 5]

HINCKLEY ROAD 1879 Hinckley in Leicestershire where John Jennings (d. 1723) became minister of the Presbyterian congregation in 1722. He removed his academy to Hinckley where a new meeting house was immediately built for him. Prior to moving to Hinckley John Jennings ran a nonconformist academy at Kibworth. His most distinguished student was Philip Doddridge. [1, 6, 7]

HOLBECK ROW 1900 (Park Row) Holbeche Hospital in the County of Lincoln. [1, 7, 37]

HOLLYDALE ROAD 1871 (Halton Terrace and Shirley Terrace) Probably an association of ideas: Hollydale and Ivydale in close proximity. [1, 4, 7]

HOLLYDALE SCHOOL 1931 See Hollydale Road. [236]

HOLLYDALE TAVERN, 115 Hollydale Road (P) See Hollydale Road.

HOLLYDENE, Acorn Estate 1963 Holly – evergreen tree. [1, 2, 26]

HOLLY GROVE 1939 (South Grove) The holly bushes in the shrubbery bordering this road. [1, 4, 8]

HOLLY GROVE SHRUBBERY See Holly Grove. The Shrubbery existed in 1875. [3, 17]

HOLME HOUSE, Studholme Street 1956 Part of street name. [172]

HOMELEIGH ROAD 1893 Origin not traced. [7]

HONEYWOOD HOUSE, Oliver Goldsmith Estate 1954 Sir William Honeywood in *The Good Natur'd Man* by Oliver Goldsmith. [1, 2, 93]

HONITON GARDENS, Gibbon Road 1961 Honiton in Devon. [5, 400]

HOOKS CLOSE, Cossall Estate 1978 Hook's Road was demolished to make way for the Cossall Estate. Hook's Road (1866) was named after Hook Lane which is shown on an 1830 map. It disappeared in 1872 when Kirkwood Road was laid out. [2, 7, 180, 212]

HOOPER HALL, Consort Road 1907 The Misses Hooper who were the wife and sister-in-law of the Vicar of St. Mary Magdalene, the Rev. Michael Biggs (1815-85) who served at St. Mary's for 21 years (1860-81). [264, 265, 340]

HOPE, 66 Rye Lane (P) In Greek mythology Pandora was given a box that she was forbidden to open. She disobeyed out of curiosity and released from it all the ills that beset man, leaving only hope within. [298, 323]

HORDLE PROMENADE EAST, NORTH, SOUTH and WEST, North Peckham Estate 1971 Hordle in Hampshire. [2, 5]

HOWARD COURT, Peckham Rye 1938 The foundation stone was laid by Peggy and Pat Hopwood, the twin daughters of the owner, but no record has been found of who Howard was. [364, 365]

HOWBURY MISSION 1892 See Howbury Road. Formerly a mission chapel connected with Peckham Rye Congregational Church and now run by the London City Mission. [340, 351]

HOWBURY ROAD 1877 Probably Howbury at Slade Green in the London Borough of Bexley. [1, 4, 7]

HOWDEN STREET 1876 Possibly after Howden in Humberside. [1, 5, 7]

HOYLAND CLOSE, Ledbury Estate 1965 and 1969 Upper Hall Street became Hoyland Road in 1934. This was near where Hoyland Close was built. Hoyland Road may have been named after the 18th century poet Francis Hoyland. [1, 2, 6, 8, 20]

HUDDERSFIELD HOUSE, Sumner Estate 1938 Huddersfield Canal. [1, 2, 108]

HUGUENOT SQUARE 1978 Built close to where Huguenot Road (1878- formerly Cadenham Road) used to be. The de Crespigny family owned land in this area. Huguenots were French Protestants of the 16th and 17th centuries. Civil rights were granted to the Huguenots by Henry IV of France in the Edict of Nantes (1598). After the revocation of the Edict by Louis XIV in 1685 very many Huguenots fled to Britain. Claude Champion de Crespigny (b. 17 May 1620) was an officer of high rank in the French service but at the revocation of the Edict of Nantes he left France with the whole of his family and came to England. [1, 7, 21, 26, 47, 361]

HYNDMAN'S STREET Henry Mayers Hyndman (1842-1921), social writer and politician. [1, 6]

I

ILDERTON ROAD 1879 Ilderton in Northumberland or Lucy and Nancy Ilderton in *The Black Dwarf* by Sir Walter Scott. [1, 5, 7, 90]

INDUS COURT, Garnies Close 1971 River Indus, Pakistan. [26, 361]

INVERTON ROAD 1886 Inverton in Highland. [7, 283]

IVYDALE ROAD 1882 Ivydale: dale = valley between hills i.e. between Nunhead and Telegraph Hills. [7, 350]

IVYDALE SCHOOL 1898 See Ivydale Road. [340, 381]

J

JACK JONES HOUSE, 12 Reedham Street Jack Jones (1913-), general secretary of the Transport and General Workers' Union from 1969 until 1978, opened this accommodation for pensioners on 2 July 1987. [95, 109, 110, 111, 112, 113, 114, 115, 116]

JARVIS HOUSE, Oliver Goldsmith Estate 1955 Jarvis in *The Good Natur'd Man* by Oliver Goldsmith. [1, 2, 93]

JAY OPTICIANS, Aylesham Centre, Rye Lane (B) Leslie Stuart Isaac Jay started in Peckham as an Opthalmic Optician in 1930, trading as Leslie S. Jay (Opticians) Ltd. on the first and second floors of 5 Central Buildings, Rye Lane. He had a uniformed commissionaire standing by the entrance promoting the practice. Leslie Jay died in April 1976. Since June 1987 the firm has traded as Jay Opticians. [228]

J. F. AYRE, Master Bakers, 131/133 Evelina Road (B) John Frederick Ayre opened the bakery business on its present site in 1955. He was known as Fred the Bread. The Ayre family's baking tradition goes back seven generations to the early 1800s. [224]

JOHN CARTER HOUSE, 25 Commercial Way In June 1968 John Carter became Senior General Foreman for the North Peckham Project, which was a small unit of Southwark Council responsible for building the North Peckham Estate. After the completion of the Estate, John Carter was involved in many other projects for Southwark. At the time of his death in February 1981 he was the Contracts Manager for Southwark Construction. In view of the high esteem in which John Carter was held by his colleagues, management and Members of the Council, it was decided in the late Autumn of 1981 to designate the office complex "John Carter House" as a fitting memorial to the man and his work. [174]

JOHN DONNE SCHOOL, Wood's Road Opened as Wood's Road School in 1881. John Donne. See *Who Was Who in Peckham.* [17, 349]

JOWETT STREET 1938 (Middle Street) Benjamin Jowett (1817-93) was master of Balliol College, Oxford. He was born in the parish of Camberwell on 15 April 1817. [3, 6, 8]

J. SAINSBURY, Moncrieff Street John James Sainsbury (1844-1928) opened his first shop at 173 Drury Lane in 1869. Prior to houses being demolished to make way for the store which opened in 1982 and closed on 13 March 1993, Sainsbury's had a shop at 61-63 Rye Lane. This was opened on 6 November 1931. When it closed on 27 November 1982 it was Sainsbury's last old-type shop where staff served customers over the counter. [41, 259, 260, 261, 262, 263, 396]

K

KAREN COURT, 25-27 Peckham Hill Street c. 1955 Origin not traced. [322]

KELLIES (formerly Adam and Eve), 14 Peckham High Street (P) Renamed by its Irish owner who wanted an Irish-sounding name. [275]

KELVINGTON ROAD 1894 Possibly a misspelling of Kilvington in Nottinghamshire or Yorkshire. [1, 5, 7]

KEMBLE COURT, Gloucester Grove Estate 1976 Kemble in Gloucestershire. [2, 5]

KENNET HOUSE, Sumner Estate 1951 Kennet and Avon Canal. [1, 2, 177]

KENTMERE HOUSE, Tustin Estate 1965 Kentmere in Cumbria. [2, 5]

KENT WAY, Camden Estate 1976 Close to where Kent Cottages stood. [2, 7, 400]

KESTON ROAD 1879 Presumably Keston in the London Borough of Bromley. [1, 5, 7]

KETLEY HOUSE, Sumner Estate 1953 Ketley Canal. [1, 2, 69]

KILMESTON WAY, North Peckham Estate 1971 Kilmeston in Hampshire. [2, 5]

KIMBERLEY AVENUE 1936 (Selborne Terrace, Stanley Terrace; Kimberley Road from 1867 and 1872 respectively) Probably named in honour of John Wodehouse (1826-1902) who was created the first Earl of Kimberley in 1866. [1, 4, 6, 7, 8, 10]

KINCAID ROAD 1883 Probably after Sir John Kincaid (1787-1862) of the Rifle Brigade. He was severely wounded at Waterloo. [1, 4, 6]

KING ARTHUR CLOSE 1980-81 Built close to where King Arthur Street used to be. [21, 361]

KINGFISHER HOUSE, Pelican Estate 1964 Kingfisher. [1, 2, 120]

KING JOHN, 45 Peckham High Street (P) There is a tradition that King John killed a stag while hunting at Peckham. [3]

KINGSBURY HOUSE, 777 Old Kent Road Foundation stone laid by Mary Smith on 18 January 1973. Origin not traced. [397]

KINGS GROVE 1938 (King's Road; prior to 1872 Somerset Villas and Brooklyn Villas) Association of ideas: Kings Grove off Queen's Road. [1, 4, 7, 8]

KINGS ON THE RYE, 132 Peckham Rye (P) Formerly King's Arms. Blanch (1875) wrote: "John Barleycorn is proverbially loyal, and therefore ... we have 'The King's Arms' (Peckham Rye)". [3, 11, 291, 292]

KINSALE ROAD 1907 Kinsale near Cork (association with Peckham unknown). [1, 7]

KIRKWOOD ROAD 1868 (Henry's Cottages, Sunnyside Cottages, Chichester Terrace, Melrose Cottages) Kirkwood, place and house 4½ miles S.S.W. of Lockerbie, Dumfries and Galloway in Scotland. [1, 5, 7, 27]

KNOTTINGLEY HOUSE, Sumner Estate 1951 Knottingley Canal. [1, 2, 108]

L

LABURNUM CLOSE, Brimmington Estate 1979 A laburnum tree stood in the Close until it was cut down in about 1990. [2, 377]

LAGAN HOUSE, Sumner Estate 1953 Lagan Navigation from Belfast to Lough Neagh. [1, 2, 42]

LAMBROOK HOUSE, Clifton Estate 1969 Lambrook in Somerset. [2, 5]

LANBURY ROAD 1887 Origin not traced. [7]

LANCEFIELD HOUSE, Nunhead Estate 1950 Mr. Lancefield was one of the principal coachmasters in the parish of Camberwell at the beginning of the 19th century. [1, 2,3]

LANDPORT WAY, North Peckham Estate 1971 Landport, a district of Portsmouth in Hampshire. [2, 5]

LANE WARD See Rye Lane.

LANVANOR ROAD 1877 Origin not traced. [7]

LASBOROUGH COURT, Gloucester Grove Estate 1975 Lasborough in Gloucestershire. [2, 5]

LATONA ROAD 1879 Latona is Latin for Leto who was a Titaness, the daughter of Coeus and Phoebe, the mother of Apollo and Artemis. [7, 336]

LATTER-RAIN OUTPOURING REVIVAL BETHANY, Copleston Road This black pentecostal church took over Church House, built in 1902 for St. Saviour's, in 1984. The Latter-Rain Outpouring Revival was established in

London in 1965 by Bishop Olive V. Parris, D.D., Ph.D., a former Salvation Army officer in the West Indies. The origin of the name goes back to the day the Lord spoke to her, as a young evangelist, that there would be an "outpouring of the latter rain which will be more glorious than the former rain". [266, 267]

LAUSANNE ROAD 1874 (part of Cemetery Road, Carlton Terrace, Rose Villas, Stanley Villas, Laburnham Villas, Clifton Villas, Leicester Villas, Clarendon Villas, Lausanne Villas) Lausanne in Switzerland. [1, 7]

LAWN PLACE, Camden Estate 1976 Lawn Houses used to be in Peckham Road. [2, 3]

LEAH HOUSE, 55a Chadwick Road (B) 1991 Workshop of clothing manufacturer Leah Leisurewear. The girl's name Leah was chosen at random for registration at Companies House. [238, 343]

LEDBURY ESTATE 1965-69 See Ledbury Street. [2]

LEDBURY STREET 1863 Ledbury in Hereford and Worcester. [1, 5, 7]

LEEDS HOUSE, Sumner Estate 1937 Leeds and Liverpool Canal. [1, 2, 108]

LEONTINE CLOSE, Bells Gardens Estate 1980 Leontine in *The Good Natur'd Man* by Oliver Goldsmith. [2, 93, 400]

LEO STREET 1879 (Charles Street, Charles Cottages, Linden Terrace, Carleton Terrace) A humorous allusion to Washington Lyon, a Camberwell Vestryman who lived in Asylum Road. Lyon was still living at the time the street was named so approval of "Lyon Street" was withheld. [1, 3, 7, 10]

LEWES HOUSE, Friary Estate 1937 Franciscan community at Lewes in East Sussex. [1, 37, 308, 361]

LEYTON SQUARE PARK Leyton Square Garden, as it was originally called, was opened in 1901. Probably named after Leyton in East London. [1, 4]

LIDDLE WARD Alice Gertrude Liddle, a Councillor for eighteen years, who died in King's College Hospital on 2 December 1975, her 73rd birthday. She was first elected as a member of the Metropolitan Borough of Camberwell for Clifton Ward in May 1953. Subsequently Miss Liddle was re-elected in 1956, 1959 and 1962.

After the amalgamation of the boroughs in 1965, she was elected as Councillor for Brunswick Ward of the London Borough of Southwark. For about 35 years Miss Liddle worked as agent and later as secretary for the Peckham branch of the Labour Party. [319, 320]

LIMERICK HOUSE, Sumner Estate 1939 Limerick Canal in Ireland. [1, 2]

LIMESFORD ROAD 1884 In company with Linden Grove which borders the north side of Nunhead Cemetery. Linden = another name for lime tree. [7, 350]

LIMES WALK, Linden Grove 1970-71 Lime is the British name for the linden trees of the genus *Tilia*. [2, 26]

LINDEN GROVE 1889 (Linden Terrace, Lyel Terrace, Clifton Villas, Oxford Villas, Cambridge Villas, Tresco Terrace) A grove of lime trees. Twenty-four lime trees were planted to lead from the main entrance gates of Nunhead Cemetery to the chapel. [1, 4, 7, 145]

LINDEN GROVE ESTATE 1947-1980 See Linden Grove. [2]

LINDLEY ESTATE 1950-69 John Lindley (1799-1865), botanist and horticulturist. All blocks of flats are named after botanists in honour of Peter Collinson, the Quaker botanist of Peckham. [1, 2, 6, 17]

LINWOOD WAY, North Peckham Estate 1971 Linwood in Hampshire. [2, 25]

LISFORD STREET 1876 (Bath Place, Elizabeth Street) Origin not traced. [7]

LISMORE HOUSE, Linden Grove Estate 1948 Lismore, Scottish island known as the Great Garden. [1, 2, 179]

LISS WAY, North Peckham Estate 1971 Liss in Hampshire. [2, 5]

LISTER HEALTH CENTRE, 1 Camden Square Joseph Lister (1827-1912) who became Lord Lister of Lyme Regis. He was Professor of Clinical Surgery at King's College (1877-93). Lister Health Centre was officially opened on 2 February 1978 by Sir John Donne, chairman of the South-East Thames Regional Health Authority. [6, 71, 72, 73, 74]

LIVESEY, Tustin Street This residential home for elderly people was named after the Livesey family who were great benefactors to Southwark. Mr. Thomas Livesey, manager and secretary of the South Metropolitan Gas Company (1839-42), was a warm friend and liberal patron of local charities. His son, Sir George Livesey who became chairman, was instrumental in establishing the Working Men's Club and was donor of the Livesey Library in 1890. See Ullswater House. [49]

LIVESEY MUSEUM, 682 Old Kent Road Opened on 30 March 1974. Erected in 1890 as the first public library in Camberwell; the gift of Sir George Livesey. See *Who Was Who in Peckham.* [17,382]

LIVESEY PLACE 1926 (Elizabeth Cottages) Sir George Livesey. See above. [1, 8, 17]

LOANDA HOUSE, Linden Grove Estate 1948 Loanda, former name of Luanda, seaport capital of Angola, SW Africa. The three oldest blocks on this estate – Linden, Lismore and Loanda – all bear the name of harbours. [1, 2, 219]

LODER STREET 1874 (York Grove North and Clifton Cottages) Probably in honour of James Loader, Camberwell Vestryman (1863). [1, 7, 128]

LONDON AND BRIGHTON, 154 Asylum Road (P) Close to former London, Brighton and South Coast Railway line. [4, 21]

LONDON WILDLIFE GARDEN CENTRE, Marsden Road Opened in December 1989 by the London Wildlife Trust in a disused Southwark Council yard. [399]

LONGHOPE CLOSE, Gloucester Grove Estate Longhope in Gloucestershire. [5]

LORD LYNDHURST, 53 Lyndhurst Way (P) See Lyndhurst Grove. [3, 294]

LUGARD ROAD 1877 (Gurdon Road) Rt. Hon. Sir Edward Lugard (1810-98). Entered army 1828; General, 1872; served Afghan War, 1842; Sikh War, 1845-46; Punjab Campaign, 1848-49; Persian War, 1856-57; Under-Secretary War Department, 1861-71. [1, 4, 7, 10, 32]

LULWORTH ROAD 1877 Lulworth in Dorset. [1, 5, 7]

LYDNEY CLOSE, Gloucester Grove Estate Lydney in Gloucestershire. [5]

LYMPSTONE GARDENS, Lindley Estate 1963-69 Lympstone in Devon. [1, 2, 5]

LYNBROOK CLOSE, Gloucester Grove Estate 1974 Lydbrook in Gloucestershire. (Spelling may have been changed to avoid confusion with nearby Lydney Close.) [5, 400]

LYNDHURST GROVE 1877 (Grove Terrace and Andover Terrace) John Singleton Copley (1772-1863), who was created Baron Lyndhurst. A lawyer, he was Solicitor General 1819-24, Attorney General 1824-26 and Lord Chancellor in 1827. [1, 6, 10]

LYNDHURST SQUARE 1843 See Lyndhurst Grove. [144]

LYNDHURST WAY 1938 (Lyndhurst Road) See Lyndhurst Grove. [1, 4, 8]

LYNN HOUSE, Friary Estate 1937 Franciscan community at Lynn in Norfolk. [1, 5, 14, 37, 361]

M

MACHELL ROAD 1877 Probably James Octavius Machell (1837-1902), owner and manager of racehorses. Three of his own horses won the Grand National Steeplechase in 1873, 1874 and 1876. [1,6, 7]

MAGDALENE CLOSE 1981 Proximity to St. Mary Magdalene School. Mary Magdalene was a disciple of Jesus. [127, 361]

MAISMORE ARMS, 104 Peckham Park Road (P) See Maismore Street.

MAISMORE STREET 1910 (Maismore Terrace and William's Cottages) Maismore Terrace. Maismore Square is shown on Dewhirst's 1842 map. [7, 143]

MALLARD HOUSE, Pelican Estate 1956 Mallard. [1, 2, 120]

MANATON CLOSE 1980 Built partly on the site of Manaton Road (1868). Probably named after Manaton in Devon. [1, 7, 21, 361]

MAN OF KENT, 2 Nunhead Green (P) Traditionally the description of a man born to the east of the River Medway, while those born to the west of it claim the title of Kentish Man. Probably chosen in contrast to the local commemoration of the Maid of Kent. See Barton Close. [295, 340]

MANOR COURT, 43 Talfourd Road 1960 There was no particular reason why this name was chosen. [322, 337]

MANOR GROVE 1879 (Hall's Cottages, Whittmee's Cottages, Victoria Place) Hatcham Manor. [1, 7, 61]

MARCUS HOUSE, Peckham High Street 1933 Built by Church Army Housing Ltd. A good benefactor to this housing scheme was a person called Marcus. [242, 243, 244]

MARLBOROUGH HEAD, 74 Marmont Road (P) Marmont Road used to be Marlborough Road. [7]

MARMONT ROAD 1882 (Marlborough Road) Probably Auguste Frédéric Louis Viesse de Marmont (1774-1854), Marshal of France. [7, 26]

MARNE HOUSE, Sumner Estate 1954 Marne Canal in France. [1, 2, 26]

MARSDEN ROAD 1884 (Harrison Villas, Lee Villas, Elizabeth Villas, Ferndale Villas, Carisbrooke Villas, Branscombe Villas, Stanley Villas) George William Marsden (1812-93) lived at 113 Camberwell Grove. He was elected vestry clerk of Camberwell in 1852. [1, 3, 7, 10, 135]

MARTOCK COURT, Clifton Estate 1967 Martock in Somerset. [2, 5]

MATTINGLEY WAY, North Peckham Estate 1971 Mattingley in Hampshire. [2, 5]

MAXTED ROAD 1876 (Blenklow Terrace, Woodlands Terrace, Winster Terrace, Bonsall Terrace, Hazelwood Terrace) Probably Maxted Street, a Kent hamlet. [1, 5, 7]

MAXDEN COURT, Maxted Road 1962 Variation on name of road. [172]

MAYFAIR COURT, Fenwick Road 1963 Private estate named by the builders whose offices were in Mayfair. [1]

McCABE'S TAVERN, 107 Sumner Road (P) Mathew McCabe, owner since 31 March 1992. [307]

McDERMOTT ROAD Bryan McDermott, landowner c. 1830. [1, 10]

McKERRELL ROAD 1878 (Wadham Road) McKerrell was the maiden name of Lady Claude Champion de Crespigny. She was the second daughter of Robert McKerrell. Sir Claude married Georgiana Louisa Margaret McKerrell on 19 September 1872. [1, 3, 7, 47, 148]

MEDINA HOUSE, Rye Hill Estate 1959 River Medina, Isle of Wight. [1, 2, 5]

MEETING HOUSE LANE An old name marked on Rocque's map of 1744. The original meeting house of the congregation which later became known as Hanover Chapel was in this lane. [1, 3, 4, 10, 67]

MELON ROAD 1906 (Martins Road, Melon Place, Britannia Place, Britannia Cottages, Britannia Terrace, Melon Cottages) Site of a 17th century melon ground, on part of Basing Manor. Sir Thomas Gardyner, who lived at Basing Manor House, sent King Charles I some melons. [1, 3, 7, 10]

MERSEY HOUSE, Sumner Estate 1939 Mersey and Irwell Navigation. [1, 2, 77]

MERTTINS ROAD 1886 Origin not traced. [7]

MILFORD WAY, Camden Estate 1976 Milford Cottages were demolished when the Camden Estate was built. [2, 7, 400]

MILLBROOK HOUSE, Friary Estate 1952 Millbrook Priory, Bedfordshire. [1, 308]

MISSION PLACE 1936 (Blue Anchor Lane) Orchard Mission, opened in 1906. [8, 129]

MITCHELDEAN COURT, Gloucester Grove Estate 1976 Mitcheldean in Gloucestershire. [2, 5]

MONCRIEFF ESTATE 1978 See Moncrieff Street. [2]

MONCRIEFF STREET 1871 (Cambridge Terrace) Sir Alexander Moncrieff (1829-1906), colonel and engineer. He was a designer of gun mechanisms. The street was named in the year that he was elected a Fellow of the Royal Society. [1, 4, 6, 10]

MONKLAND HOUSE, Camden Estate 1949 Monkland Canal, Scotland. [1, 8, 42]

MONTAGUE SQUARE 1981-82 Origin not traced. [361]

MONTEAGLE WAY 1979 Lord Monteagle (1790-1866), patron of the Metropolitan Beer and Wine Society. He laid the first stone of the Society's asylum at Nunhead Green in 1852. [2, 3, 6, 180]

MONTPELIER, 43 Choumert Road (P) Choumert Road used to be Montpelier Road. [7, 296]

MONTPELIER, 99 Queen's Road (P) c. 1853 On the corner of Montpelier Road. [144, 296]

MONTPELIER ROAD 1875 (Wellington Villas) Montpellier (sic.) in France was seat of an ancient university and medical school and virtually the only malaria-free cultural centre on the Mediterranean. It was a favourite destination for young British aristocrats and their tutors doing the Grand Tour of Europe during the 17th and early 18th centuries. By the early 19th century, when the British streets were built, Montpellier was no longer favoured by well-heeled British tourists who were transferring their affections to Nice and Monte Carlo, but the aristocratic association persisted and the speculative builders and developers who "ran up" the new terraces and streets for their middle class clients naturally chose an upmarket name with aristocratic pretensions.

What is unclear is why invariably the street name is misspelt, "Montpelier" (one L), unless the builders were trying to save a little on the cast iron of the street signage. [1, 7, 318]

MORNING STAR, 231 Rye Lane (P) The planet Venus when visible in the East before sunrise. [210]

MORTLOCK CLOSE, Cossall Estate 1977-78 Before the Cossall Estate was built, Mortlock Gardens (1869) stood where part of Cossall Park is today. Part of Harder's Road used to be known as Mortlock Terrace. [1, 7, 21]

MOTHER GOOSE NURSERY SCHOOL, 34 Waveney Avenue The way a mother goose looks after her goslings prompted the use of this name for a nursery school. [221, 222]

MURDOCK STREET 1938 (Alexander Street) William Murdock (1754-1839), engineer and inventor of coal-gas lighting. [1, 6, 8, 10]

MUSCHAMP ROAD 1877 Muschamp family, prominent in Camberwell and Peckham from c.1500 to c.1670 when their estates were bought by Sir Thomas Bond. There is a memorial to Thomas Muschamp in St. Giles' Church, Camberwell. [1, 3, 7, 10, 130]

N

NAILSWORTH COURT, Gloucester Grove Estate 1976 Nailsworth in Gloucestershire. [2, 7]

NAYLOR ROAD 1863 (Exon Terrace, Pembroke Cottages, Milford Grove, Milford Cottages) Elizabeth Caroline Naylor, of 15 The Gardens, who leased six houses in Naylor Road in 1877. [4, 7, 137]

NELL GWYN NURSERY SCHOOL, Staffordshire Street 1935 Nell Gwyn. See *Who Was Who in Peckham.* [17, 354]

NEVILLE CLOSE, Bells Gardens Estate 1980 Miss Constance Neville in *She Stoops to Conquer* by Oliver Goldsmith. [2, 23, 93, 400]

NEWENT CLOSE, Gloucester Grove Estate 1972 Newent in Gloucestershire. [2, 9]

NEW JAMES COURT, Nunhead Lane 1966 Built on part of the site of New James Street. [181, 361]

NEW JAMES STREET ESTATE 1957-78 See New James Court. [2]

NEWLANDS The last part of Nunhead to be built on at the turn of the century. [340]

NIGEL ROAD 1872 Possibly *The Fortunes of Nigel* by Sir Walter Scott. [1, 7, 23]

NILE TERRACE The Battle of the Nile (1798). [10, 131]

NORTHFIELD HOUSE, Friary Estate 1934 North Field was a plot of land that bordered the Peckham Manor. [1, 2]

NORTHLEACH COURT, Gloucester Grove Estate 1976 Northleach in Gloucestershire. [2, 5]

NORTH PECKHAM BAPTIST CHURCH, East Surrey Grove Opened in 1880 as James's Grove Baptist Church. See East Dulwich Baptist Church. [3, 352]

NORTH PECKHAM ESTATE 1950-72 See Peckham. [2]

NUNHEAD It was not until the Tudor or Elizabethan eras that there emerged the place name of "Nonehead". The name is said to have originated from the beheading of the Mother Superior of a nunnery on the site of the old Nun's Head pub, who opposed Henry VIII's anti-monastic plans – her severed head being placed on a pike at Nunhead Green for all to see. The name Nunhead is first shown on John Rocque's map dated 1741-45 and again on a map of 1754. [44, 369]

NUNHEAD CEMETERY Consecrated by the Bishop of Winchester on 29 July 1840. See Nunhead. [289]

NUNHEAD CRESCENT 1894 (William's Terrace). See Nunhead. [1, 7]

NUNHEAD ESTATE 1950-56 See Nunhead. [2]

NUNHEAD GREEN See Nunhead. Camberwell Vestry bought Nunhead Green in 1868 for £1,000 on condition that it remained open to the public in perpetuity. [4]

NUNHEAD GROVE 1889 (Nunhead Terrace, Daniel's Cottages, Montague Villas, Florence Villas) See Nunhead. [7]

NUNHEAD HILL 200 feet above sea level. See Nunhead. [340]

NUNHEAD LANE 1889 (Beaufort Terrace, Philbrick Terrace, James Place, Belle Vue Terrace, Osborne Villas, Percy Terrace, Cambridge Terrace, Elm Place, Adelaide Terrace, Renfrew Terrace, York Place) See Nunhead. [7, 10]

NUTBROOK STREET 1876 (Parson's Villas, Colville Terrace, Roseley Terrace, Eccleston Terrace) Local field name. [1, 7, 10]

NUTCROFT ROAD 1875 Local field name. [1, 4, 7]

NUTT STREET 1873 (Charles Street) Joseph Nutt, Surveyor of Highways 1700-75. [1, 7]

O

OAKDALE ROAD 1980 (Ivydale Road) Renamed in company with Hollydale Road and its former name. [180]

OAKDENE, Acorn Estate 1962 Oak tree. Dene means vale. [1, 2, 19]

OGLANDER ROAD 1877 (Colville Grove, Wildash Road, Leyton Terrace, Oglander Terrace, Frederick Terrace, Thompson Villas Frenchwood Villas, Withernsea Villas, Avenham Villas, Walton Villas, Fern Villas, Myrtle Villas, Oak Villas, Ash Villas, Elm Villas, Birch Villas) Sir John Oglander (1585-1655), diarist. He married Sir Thomas Grymes' sister, Frances, on 4 August 1606. [1, 4, 6, 7, 10]

OLD JAMES STREET 1966 Possibly William James, Surveyor to Dulwich College property, early 19th century. [1, 361]

OLD KENT ROAD The road leading from London to Kent, dating back to the Romans. [1, 4, 10]

OLD NUN'S HEAD, 15 Nunhead Green (P) 1934 See Nunhead. [44]

OLIVER GOLDSMITH ESTATE 1930-59 Oliver Goldsmith. See *Who Was Who in Peckham.* [2, 17]

ONDINE ROAD 1876 (Rutland Villas, Mount Villas, Aden Villas, Pine Villas, Crescent Villas, Dartmouth Villas, Tiverton Villas, Buxton Villas, Salisbury Villas, Bexley Villas, Brookwood Villas, Argyle Villas, Lorne Villas, Luton Villas, Charlton Villas, Hatherley Villas, Belmont Villas, Clarence Villas, Ryde Villas, Ventnor Villas, Merton Villas, Camden Villas, Florence Villas, Clifton Villas, Rosedale Villas, Taunton Villas, Brighton Villas, Shanklin Villas, Lonsdale Villas, Pevensey Villas, Westbury Villas, Clyde Villas, Clevedon Villas, Wellington Villas, Marlborough Villas, Litchurch Villas) Ondine, or Undine, the water nymph in *Undine* by Fouqué (Friedrich Heinrich Karl), Baron de la Motte (1777-1843), German poet. *Undine* was published in 1811 and adapted as a play by Jean Giraudoux *(Ondine,* 1939). [1, 7, 23, 132]

OPHIR TERRACE 1901 (York Terrace, Acacia Terrace) Ophir, a region celebrated in ancient times for its fine gold and frequently mentioned in the Old Testament. Its position has been the subject of much dispute. [7, 26]

ORMSIDE STREET 1874 (St. James's Street, Grove Cottages, Stafford Place, St. Thomas's Terrace, Alpha Cottages, Oxford Place, St. Ann's Place, Sarah's Place) Great Ormside in Cumbria. [1, 5, 7]

OSPREY HOUSE, Pelican Estate 1957 Osprey. [1, 2, 120]

OXENFORD STREET 1902 Playwright John Oxenford (1812-77) who was born in Camberwell. [1, 3, 7, 10]

P

PAINSWICK COURT, Gloucester Grove Estate 1976 Painswick in Gloucestershire. [2, 5]

PALYNS HOUSE, 270 Consort Road George Palyn, Master of the Girdlers Company in 1595. In 1610 he gave money by Will to found his Almshouse Charity. [28]

PARKSIDE NEIGHBOURHOOD HOUSING OFFICE, 27 Bournemouth Road 1991 Bournemouth Road neighbourhood forum decided to change the name of the neighbourhood office to Parkside to reflect the number of parks in the area and the greener aspect of Peckham. [237]

PARKSTONE ROAD 1866 Parkstone in Dorset. [4, 5, 7]

PATCHWAY COURT, Gloucester Grove Estate 1976 Patchway in Avon. [2, 5]

PATTERDALE ROAD 1965 Patterdale in Cumbria. [2, 5]

PECKHAM Old English *Peac-ham* – village by a hill. We cannot be sure which hill – Nunhead Hill, Telegraph Hill or Honor Oak Hill? Manorial and other evidence strongly suggests that it was Nunhead Hill. Here stood the original Manor of Bredinghurst which may be identified with "lands of Pecheham" belonging to Bishop Maminot at the time of the Domesday Survey. Peckham was called Pecheha in Domesday Book. [3, 44, 133, 368, 369]

PECKHAM CHRISTIAN FELLOWSHIP, Consort Road. Ichthus use the former St. Paul's Church opened in 1907. St. Paul (d. c. A.D. 65) was an apostle of Jesus Christ. [284, 287]

PECKHAM GROVE 1867 (Cambridge Terrace) See Peckham. [7]

PECKHAM HIGH STREET The high or principal street. See Peckham. [10]

PECKHAM HILL STREET 1939 (Hill Street and originally Lord's Lane) Mrs. Martha Hill. See *Who Was Who in Peckham.* [1, 8, 10, 17]

PECKHAM METHODIST CHURCH, Wood's Road 1974 John Wesley, founder of Methodism, was leader of a group of friends at Oxford who read the Bible and prayed regularly together. When the group's activities became known, derisive undergraduates called it various names including "The Enthusiasts", "The Bible Moths" and "The Holy Club" but the name which stuck was the "Methodists" (presumably given because of the curiously methodical way of life which they followed). [43, 142]

PECKHAM PARK ROAD 1870 (Park Road, Charles Place, Mary's Place, Leah Cottages, Nile Terrace, Cambridge Terrace, Lebanon Place, Sutherland Terrace, Eagle Place, Trafalgar Place, Clyde Cottages, Gloucester Cottages, Gloucester Place, Park Villas, Henry's Cottages, Villa Place, William Cottages, Maismore Place, Park Terrace, George Terrace, Edwin Place). Before the growth of the area in the 19th century this area was known as Peckham Park. Blanch states that it was "a park of considerable extent". Park Road was formerly called Peckham Gap. [1, 3, 4, 7, 10, 190]

PECKHAM PARK ROAD BAPTIST CHURCH, Peckham Park Road Opened on 5 May 1951. See above and East Dulwich Baptist Church. [288]

PECKHAM PARK SCHOOL, Friary Road Opened on 4 September 1876 as Lower Park Road School. See Peckham Park Road. [302]

PECKHAM ROAD 1892 See Peckham. [4, 7]

PECKHAM RYE See Peckham. Rye is Old English *ripe* meaning "brook". Peckham Rye is mentioned in documents as early as the fourteenth century. Peckham Rye is rhyming slang for tie. [3, 4, 10, 44, 133, 136]

PECKHAM RYE PARK, SE22 Opened on 14 May 1894. See Peckham Rye. [336]

PECKHAM RYE PRIMARY SCHOOL, Whorlton Road 1926 See Peckham Rye. [184]

PECKHAM RYE STATION Opened 13 August 1866. Named Peckham Rye to distinguish it from Peckham Station (later renamed Queen's Road, Peckham). [3, 138]

PECKHAM RYE TABERNACLE BAPTIST CHURCH, 55a Nigel Road 1963 See Peckham Rye and East Dulwich Baptist Church. Tabernacle was a provisional tent where the Lord met his people. (Exodus 33: 7-10). [127, 327]

PECKHAM SEVENTH DAY ADVENTIST CHURCH, 149-159 Ivydale Road Originally Waverley Park Methodist New Connexion Chapel opened in 1896. Used by Seventh Day Adventists since March 1986. A section of the Adventists who, after the expected Second Coming of Christ failed to be realized in 1844, constituted themselves as a separate body. They observe the Old Testament Sabbath, Saturday, as the weekly day of rest and praise instead of Sunday. [4, 284, 312, 326]

PELICAN ESTATE 1956-1964 An 18th century house called Pelican House stood on the site of the Camberwell Central Library (close to where Winnie Mandela House, formerly Pelican House, is today). [1, 2, 21]

PELICAN HOUSE, Peckham Road Renamed Winnie Mandela House in 1989. See Pelican Estate. When Blanch wrote *Ye Parish of Camerwell* (1875) Pelican House had "been built at least 200 years, and the pelicans, from which it derives its name, originally stood on brick pilasters at the entrance gates". [1, 3, 21, 134]

PENARTH STREET 1874 (Cross Street, John's Place) Penarth in South Glamorgan. [1, 5, 7]

PENCRAIG WAY, Ledbury Estate 1969 Pencraig in Hereford and Worcester. [2, 5]

PENNACK ROAD 1887 Charles Pennack, builder. [1, 7]

PENNETHORNE ROAD 1883 Sir James Pennethorne (1801-71), architect. [1, 4, 6, 7]

PENTRIDGE STREET 1912 (St. George's Street) Pentridge in Dorset. Robert Browning's great-grandfather lived in the parish of Pentridge. Robert Browning was born at Southampton Street, Camberwell, on 7 May 1812. [1, 5, 6, 7, 157]

PETERCHURCH HOUSE, Ledbury Estate 1966 Peterchurch in Hereford and Worcester. [2, 5]

PHILIP ROAD 1868 (Philip Terrace and Girdler's Terrace) Philip Champion de Crespigny of Champion Lodge, Camberwell, proctor of the Courts of Admiralty and Arches. [1, 7, 47]

PHILIP WALK, Consort Estate 1978 See Philip Road. [2]

PILGRIM'S WAY SCHOOL, Tustin Estate, Manor Grove 1968 Close to the route used by pilgrims travelling to Canterbury in the middle ages. [372, 373, 374, 378, 379]

PILKINGTON ROAD 1868 (Keating Road) Sir Thomas Pilkington (b. 7 December 1773), father-in-law to Sir John Tyssen Tyrrell and grandfather of Mary Tyrrell. On 1 August 1797 at Great Waltham, Essex, he married Elizabeth Anne Tufnell. He was Sheriff of Yorkshire (1798-99). He died on 9 July 1811 aged 37. [7, 328, 329]

PINEDENE, Acorn Estate 1962 Pine tree. Dene means vale. [1, 2, 19]

PITT STREET Probably William Pitt the Younger (1759-1806) who was Prime Minister (1783-1801, 1804-06). [6, 190]

POLLARDS, 171 Rye Lane (B) The firm was founded by William Waide Pollard (1866-1937) in 1892. Trading began in the present premises in 1985 though the firm had previously had shops at 110 High Street and 165 Rye Lane. [271, 272, 273]

POMEROY ESTATE 1980-82 Pomeroy in Tyrone, Northern Ireland. [1, 2, 325]

PORTBURY CLOSE, Clifton Estate 1967 Portbury in Avon. [2, 5]

POULNER WAY, North Peckham Estate 1971 Poulner in Hampshire. [2, 5]

PRIMROSE HOUSE, Oliver Goldsmith Estate 1930 Dr. Charles Primrose, the central character in *The Vicar of Wakefield* by Oliver Goldsmith. [1, 2, 90]

PRINCE ALBERT, 111 Bellenden Road (P) Consort to Queen Victoria. This part of Bellenden Road used to be Victoria Road. [21]

PRINCE OF WALES, 14 Ruby Street (P) Very common sign (nearly 100 in Greater London alone) usually refers to Edward (1841-1910), eldest son of Queen Victoria. He became Edward VII in 1901. [295]

PRINCE OF WINDSOR, 888 Old Kent Road (P) Formerly Prince of Saxe-Cobourg. The rulers of Saxon Duchies abdicated after the First World War. Windsor is the family name of the present royal house of Great Britain. [26, 303]

PRIORY COURT, Cheltenham Road 1976 Built on the site of Priory Villas. [189, 361]

PURDON HOUSE, Oliver Goldsmith Estate 1954 Edward Purdon, a friend of Oliver Goldsmith's. Purdon was either editor of *Busy Body* or a contributor. *Busy Body* was a short-lived periodical published three times a week between 9 October and 3 November 1759. [1, 2, 93]

PYROTECHNISTS ARMS, 39 Nunhead Green (P) Close to the site of Brock's firework factory. [17]

Q

QUARLEY WAY, North Peckham Estate 1971 Quarley in Hampshire. [2, 5]

QUEDGELEY COURT, Gloucester Grove Estate 1976 Quedgeley in Gloucestershire. [2, 5]

QUEEN, 101 Commercial Way (P) Queen Elizabeth I. [298, 306]

QUEEN ELIZABETH, 61 Asylum Road (P) c.1840 Queen Elizabeth I. [144, 298, 306]

QUEEN'S ROAD 1868 (Queen's Cottages, Barden Place, Pemell's Terrace, Gotha Place, Derby Place, Montpelier Terrace, Devonshire Terrace, Oriental Place, Alexander Terrace, Ebenezer Place, Alpha Place,

Montague Terrace, Hatcham Place, Holloway Terrace, Caledonian Terrace, Wyndham Place, Belvidere Villas, Union Road, Union Terrace, Bath Place, St. Mary's Terrace, Princess Terrace, Dennet Terrace, Laural Cottages, Queen's Terrace, Victoria Terrace). Originally known as Deptford Lane, the name was altered in honour of Queen Victoria who often passed along it on her way to the Naval School at New Cross (now Goldsmiths' College). [1, 3, 4, 5, 10, 190]

QUEEN'S ROAD STATION Opened 13 August 1866. Originally Peckham Station. Renamed on 1 December 1866. [3, 138]

QUENINGTON COURT, Gloucester Grove Estate 1976 Quenington in Gloucestershire. [2, 5]

R

RADNOR ROAD 1938 (Radnor Street) Probably William Pleydell-Bouverie (1779-1869), third Earl Radnor, a distinguished whig politician. [1, 6, 8]

RAILWAY TAVERN, 66 Gibbon Road (P) Close to railway in Nunhead. [184].

RAUL ROAD 1882 Claude Raul Champion de Crespigny b. 19 September 1878. [1, 4, 7, 10, 47]

READING HOUSE, Friary Estate 1938 Franciscan community at Reading in Berkshire. [1, 2, 5, 14, 37, 308]

RECORD STREET 1895 Origin not traced. [7]

RED BULL, 116 Peckham High Street (P) Blanch (1875) wrote – "The Red Bull" (High Street, Peckham) is an ancient public-house sign. Alleyn, founder of Dulwich College, says in a memorandum, October 3, 1617: – "Went to 'The Red Bull', and received for the Younger Brother (a play) but £3 6s. 4d." [3, 295, 296]

RED COW, 190 Peckham High Street (P) Blanch (1875) wrote – Strange, or perhaps natural enough, the next house in the High Street to "The Red Bull" is "The Red Cow", and for 150 years at least both have lived in the same street upon the best of terms:-

"The Red Cow

Gives good milk now."

and of "The Red Bull" it was said,

"If you want a good pull,

Just step in at the Bull." [3]

REEDHAM STREET 1887 (Norfolk Street, Laburnam Cottages, Somershall Terrace, Ararat Cottages, Arthur Cottages) Reedham in Norfolk. [1, 5, 7]

RELF ROAD 1872 Probably in honour of Camberwell Vestryman John Thomas Relph. [1, 7, 10, 255]

REYNOLDS ROAD 1891 (Pancras Road, Priory Villas, St. Pancras Terrace) Jonathon C. Reynolds, Surveyor to Camberwell Vestry in the 1860s. [1, 3, 4, 7, 10, 128]

RICHLAND HOUSE, Oliver Goldsmith Estate 1954 Miss Richland in *The Good Natur'd Man* by Oliver Goldsmith. [1, 2, 90]

RISING SUN, 799 Old Kent Road (P) A common heraldic sign, referring to Edward III, Richard III and to many landed families. [295]

ROBERT HART MEMORIAL SUPPLEMENTARY SCHOOL, 5-9 Hordle Promenade East Robert B. O. Hart (1913-84) was born in Guyana. He was a lawyer and teacher who taught in Britain for more than twenty years.

In the late 1970s he became secretary of the Caribbean Teachers' Association and in that position was instrumental in formulating a Teaching and Educational project designed to be supportive of and supplementary to mainstream education provision. As part of this project, a supplementary school was established on the North Peckham Estate. After the death of Robert Hart, the school was named after its founder. [385, 386]

ROBERT KEEN CLOSE 1978 Alderman Robert James George Keene (sic.) who was on Camberwell Borough Council (1956-1965). He was a process engraver's etcher. [2, 269, 270]

ROCHDALE HOUSE, Sumner Estate 1938 Rochdale Canal. [1, 2, 77]

ROMAN WAY, Brimmington Estate 1982 Remains of Roman roads (Watling Street and London to Lewes road) lie nearby. [2, 16, 140]

ROSEMARY GARDENS, Southampton Way 1960 See Rosemary Road. [333]

ROSEMARY ROAD 1872 (North Street, Chandos Terrace, Castle Terrace, Cambria Cottages, Cromwell Villas, Ebenezer Terrace, Branch Buildings, Denmark Terrace, Hesse Terrace. Before the North Peckham Estate was built Rosemary Road extended from the west end of what is now Commercial Way.) The Old Rosemary Branch public house stood at the corner of what are now Southampton Way and Commercial Way. It was first recorded in c.1700. It is shown on Stockdale's map (1797). The grounds surrounding it were extensive; horse racing, cricket, pigeon shooting and all kinds of outdoor sports and pastimes were carried on. Rosemary was formerly an emblem of remembrance. "There's rosemary, that's for remembrance," say Ophelia. *(Hamlet,* Act iv, Scene 5). [1, 3, 7, 10, 21, 143, 144]

ROSENTHORPE ROAD 1894 Rosenthorpe: Thorpe = homestead or village. [7, 350]

ROSINA WHYATT MEMORIAL GARDEN, Highshore School, Bellenden Road The upkeep of the Memorial Garden is provided for by a fund given to the School by Miss Rosina Whyatt, Justice of the Peace, Alderman and Mayor (1954-55) of the Borough of Camberwell and for 21 years chairman of the managers of Highshore School. She died in August 1971 aged 85. [314]

ROTHER HOUSE, Rye Hill Estate 1951 River Rother. [1, 2, 92]

ROUPEL HOUSE, Sumner Estate 1953 Roupel ship canal in Belgium. [1, 2, 183]

ROYAL LONDON BUILDINGS, 644 Old Kent Road (B) The Royal London Mutual Insurance Society Limited purchased the freehold in 1896. The offices were built around the turn of the century. [393, 394]

ROYSTON HOUSE, Friary Estate 1950 Austin Canons community at Royston in Hertfordshire. [1, 2, 5, 14, 37, 308]

RUBY STREET 1876 (Church Street, St. Thomas Terrace, Bethwin Terrace, Church Place) Believed to be named after landowner's daughter. [1, 7]

RUBY TRIANGLE 1910 (Baker's Terrace and then The Triangle) See Ruby Street. [7]

RUDBECK HOUSE, Lindley Estate 1950 Oluf Rudbeck (d. 1702) Swedish botanist.[1, 2, 132]

RUSSELL COURT, Heaton Road 1980 Russell Road (1872) – now Blackpool Road. [7, 21, 180]

RYEGATES, Brayards Estate 1960 Rycotts, Ricotes, Rigates or Ryegates: a plot of land in Dulwich 16th-17th century. [1, 2, 3, 207]

RYE HILL ESTATE 1938-64 See Rye Hill Park. [2]

RYE HILL PARK 1901 (Portland Villas, Hillsboro', Hillside Villas) Built on hill overlooking Peckham Rye. [1, 7, 189]

RYE HOTEL, 31 Peckham Rye (P) Overlooks Peckham Rye. [184]

RYE LANE 1868 (South Street) The lane leading to Peckham Rye (q.v.). [1, 4, 7, 10]

RYE LANE CHAPEL Opened on 18 November 1863. See Rye Lane. [3]

RYE ROAD 1909 See Peckham Rye. [1, 7]

RYEVIEW, 110 Peckham Rye Has a view across the northern end of Peckham Rye. [184]

S

SAFEWAY, Aylesham Centre In 1962 the American supermarket chain "Safeway Stores Inc" entered the British market. In 1986 the Argyll Group PLC, whose main trading facia was Presto, showed an interest in Safeway Food Stores Ltd. and the following year Safeway became part of Argyll. In due course the Presto store in the Aylesham Centre became Safeway. [402]

SAINSBURY, J. See J. Sainsbury.

ST. ALBAN'S R.C. PRIMARY SCHOOL, Peckham Road Building opened on 26 September 1906 as County Secondary School, Peckham. St. Alban, the first English martyr. [162, 163, 338]

ST. ANTONY'S CHURCH, Nunhead Consecrated on 12 October 1957 by the Bishop of Southwark, Rt. Rev. Bertram Simpson. St. Antony of Egypt, the first Desert Father (c. 251-356 A.D.). [44]

ST. BRIAVELS COURT, Gloucester Grove Estate 1975 St. Briavels in Gloucestershire. [2, 5]

ST. FRANCIS R.C. SCHOOL, Friary Road St. Francis of Assisi. [162, 299]

ST. GEORGE'S CHURCH See Church of Saint George.

ST. GEORGE'S TERRACE, Peckham Hill Street Close to the district of St. George. [143]

ST. GEORGE'S WAY 1936 (St. George's Road) Proximity to St. George's Church, Wells Way, built in 1822-24 and disused since 1970. [1, 8, 10, 11]

ST. JAMES THE GREAT CHURCH, Elm Grove 1904 James the Great (d. A.D. 44), apostle and martyr. Described in the Gospels as the son of Zebedee and the brother of John, James was one of the three witnesses of the Transfiguration of Christ and his agony in the garden of Gethsemane. He was also the first apostle to die for the Christian faith, being put to the sword at Jerusalem by King Herod Agrippa. [248, 249]

ST. JAMES WALK, Camden Estate 1975 James's Grove and James's Street were nearby. [2, 155, 190]

ST. JOHN'S CHURCH, Meeting House Lane The parish church of St. John, Bishop of Constantinople was consecrated by Mervyn Stockwood, Lord Bishop of Southwark on 11 June 1966. The new building replaced two former churches – St. Chrysostom in Peckham Hill Street, demolished in 1963, and St. Jude destroyed by enemy action in 1940. The former was named after St. John Chrysostom who was elected archbishop of Constantinople in 398. St. John had been nicknamed "Chrysostom" (meaning "golden-mouthed") and it was thought appropriate that the new church should bear the saint's correct name rather than his nickname. [230, 231, 390, 391]

ST. LUKE'S CHURCH, North Peckham Estate Consecrated on St. Luke's Day, 18 October 1954. Evangelist. According to tradition he was the author of the Third Gospel and of the Acts of the Apostles. [284, 309]

ST. MARY MAGDALENE CHURCH, St. Mary's Road Consecrated on 3 November 1962 by the Bishop of Southwark, the Rt. Rev. Mervyn Stockwood. Her Majesty Queen Elizabeth the Queen Mother attended the Opening Service. Mary Magdalene was a disciple of Jesus Christ. The present church replaced one destroyed in 1940. [127, 287, 290]

ST. MARY MAGDALENE SCHOOL, Godman Road 1856 See above. [3, 127]

ST. MARY'S ROAD 1878 (Sophia Place, Lombardian Terrace, Lombardian Villas, New Villas, Ryde Villas) St. Mary Magdalene Church was consecrated by the Bishop of Winchester on 7 May 1841. It was destroyed by a land mine on 21 September 1940. [1, 3, 4, 7, 10, 147]

ST. SAVIOUR'S CHURCH, Copleston Road (now the Copleston Centre) Consecrated on 22 February 1881. Saint is an adjective meaning holy i.e. Holy Saviour's. There was no St. Saviour. [210, 211, 395]

ST. SILAS CHURCH, Ivydale Road 1903 A prominent early Christian disciple. He was St. Paul's companion on his first visit to Macedonia and Corinth. [4, 284]

ST. THOMAS THE APOSTLE CATHOLIC CHURCH, Hollydale Road 1905 One of the twelve apostles, known as "doubting Thomas". [127, 357]

ST. THOMAS THE APOSTLE SCHOOL, Hollydale Road 1965 See previous entry. [358]

SALISBURY TERRACE, Barset Estate 1981-82 Barset Road was formerly Salisbury Terrace. [2, 7]

SALLY MUGABE HOUSE, 69 Bellenden Road In 1993 this building was renamed after the wife of Zimbabwean President Robert Mugabe. Sally Mugabe died on 27 January 1992 aged 59. She was seriously ill for the last eleven years of her life but refused to allow this to get in the way of her active support for community programmes which earned her the unofficial title "Amau" – mother of the nation. She was patron of many projects involving child welfare and health, education, human rights and self-help for women. She made monthly visits to leprosy sufferers to ensure they had sufficient food and clothing. She went to Southwark in March 1987 and visited women's projects. She spoke on political changes in South Africa and their effect on women and children. [281, 282, 411]

SALVATION ARMY CITADEL, Gordon Road Opened in 1891, damaged by a bomb in 1940 and re-opened in 1960.

Minnie Lindsay Carpenter wrote in *William Booth* – "During the early months of 1878, William Booth was engaged on the preparation of a report of the Mission. With him were his son Bramwell and George Railton. As he walked up and down the room discussing the proofs, they came to the question which headed it: 'What is the Christian Mission?' 'A volunteer army of converted working people' Railton had written. William Booth looked over the young man's shoulder and, picking up a pen, struck out the word 'Volunteer', substituting 'Salvation'. Then he read aloud: 'The Christian Mission is a Salvation Army...' There was a moment of tense silence. The three men looked at each other and rose to their feet. A thrill passed from heart to heart. The Salvation Army! They felt they had suddenly burst upon a wonderful discovery; how great, was at the moment hid from their eyes." From 1879 the Mission notepaper was stamped with the new title. [388, 389]

SAMUEL JONES INDUSTRIAL ESTATE (B) Samuel Jones. See *Who Was Who in Peckham.* [17]

SANDGATE STREET 1908 (Caroline Street, Eliza Cottages or Place, part of Ruby Street) Sandgate in Kent. [1, 5, 7]

SANDISON STREET 1884 (Bedford Street, Victory Cottages) Maybe related to its former name. There is a place near Bedford called Sandy. [1, 7]

SARNESFIELD HOUSE, Ledbury Estate 1965 Sarnesfield in Hereford and Worcester. [2, 5]

SARTOR ROAD 1863 Mr. J. A. Dunn, who was a tailor, made an application for this road to be made on the estate of the Tailors' Labour Agency Freehold Land Society. Sartor is Latin for tailor. [1, 7, 23, 252, 253]

SASSOON HOUSE, St. Mary's Road 1932 This 5-storey block of 20 flats was a gift of Mrs. Meyer Sassoon to the Pioneer Housing Trust in memory of her son, R. E. Sassoon. It was designed by Maxwell Fry and opened by Sir Samuel Hoare. [2, 144, 176, 342]

SAUL COURT, Gloucester Grove Estate 1976 Saul in Gloucestershire. [2, 5]

SCAFFOLD HOUSE, Consort Road (B) Office of D & R Scaffold Group. [184]

SCIPIO STREET 1879 (George Street) John Francis Scipio, Camberwell Vestryman. [1, 3, 7]

SCYLLA ROAD 1872 (Sherlock Road, Nunhead Passage (part), Scylla Gardens, Monks Cottages, Francis Place, Scylla Terrace, Winter's Buildings, Percy Cottages) H. M. S. Scylla was the ship commanded by Captain Augustus James de Crespigny. He was renowned for his bravery in rescuing fellow sailors from drowning. He served under Nelson and Collingwood. He died on board H.M.S. Scylla on 24 October 1825 and was buried in Port Royal, Jamaica, where there is a memorial to him. [1, 7, 47, 148]

SENATE STREET 1866 Origin not traced. [7]

SHAKESPEARE COURT, 22A Peckham Rye 1990 Dramatist and poet William Shakespeare (1564-1616). [6, 215]

SHANKLIN WAY, North Peckham Estate 1971 Shanklin on the Isle of Wight. [2, 5]

SHANNON COURT, Garnies Close 1972 River Shannon, longest river in Ireland. [26, 361]

SHARPNESS COURT, Gloucester Grove Estate 1976 Sharpness in Gloucestershire. [2, 5]

SHEFFIELD HOUSE, Bellenden Road 1933 Built by Church Army Housing Ltd. A good benefactor to this housing scheme was a lady living in Sheffield. [1, 171, 242, 243, 244]

SHELLEY CLOSE, Gordon Road 1989 Poet Percy Bysshe Shelley (1792-1822). [6, 201]

SHERGAR (formerly Prince Albert), 119 Consort Road (P) Race horse Shergar won The Derby in 1981. Proprietor Joseph Beattie chose the name as he was a racing fan. [274]

SHURLAND GARDENS, Willowbrook Estate 1962 Shurland in Kent. [2, 283]

SIDMOUTH ARMS, 102 Bird-in-Bush Road (P) c. 1860 Sidmouth in Devon. [5, 144]

SIDMOUTH HOUSE, Lindley Estate 1965 Sidmouth in Devon. [1, 2, 5]

SIDMOUTH ROAD, Camden Estate 1976 Sidmouth Terrace was demolished when the Camden Estate was built. [2, 7, 400]

SISTER MABEL'S WAY 1984 Probably Sister Mabel who founded Sister Mabel's Free Dispensary for Sick Animals of the Poor of South London. She was Mabel Strangeways Hounsell, a niece of the Earl of Ilchester. She went to Camberwell to work as a housekeeper to Dr. Jarvise who practised at 325 Southampton Street. In 1921, ten years after going to Camberwell, the need for a free dispensary for animals was felt to be acute. No such service existed and people could not afford to pay the fees of veterinary surgeons. An outbuilding was fitted up and pets were treated by a veterinary surgeon while Sister Mabel treated the owners. She died in October 1927. The Dispensary was moved to 1 Camberwell Station Road. [2, 166, 167]

SKENFRITH HOUSE, Ledbury Estate 1965 Skenfrith in Gwent – close to Hereford and Worcester border. [2, 5]

SMITH, W. H. See W. H. Smith.

SOAMES STREET 1873 (Gloucester Terrace, Soames Villas, Soames Terrace, Lavington Terrace) Soames Villas and Soames Terrace. [1, 6, 7]

SOJOURNER TRUTH ASSOCIATION, 161 Sumner Road Uses former St. Luke's Primary School built in c. 1845. Sojourner Truth (c. 1797-1883).

American abolitionist. She was born a slave and belonged to several owners before working on a farm in New York State (1810-26). Here she had at least eight children by a fellow slave Thomas, but in 1827 she fled to another farm owned by the Van Wagener family. She successfully fought a legal battle to obtain the freedom of her son, illegally sold to an Alabama planter, and after receiving her own freedom moved to New York as Isabella van Wagener.

During the next 15 years she worked in the city, becoming involved with various visionary groups, until in 1843 she was commanded by voices to leave and take the name Sojourner Truth. She spoke at revival meetings in the Eastern states, and in 1847 met leading abolitionists in Northampton, Massachusetts. In 1850 she went west, selling her biography, *The Narrative of Sojourner Truth,* drawing huge crowds by her dramatic lectures on slavery and, increasingly, on the suffrage issue. She eventually settled in Battle Creek, Michigan, worked for union causes, was received by Lincoln in 1864, and became a worker for the Freedman's Relief Association. Her last campaigns were for land grants and a 'Negro state', and she encouraged Negro emigration to the Midwest. When she finally retired in 1875 she continued to receive visitors from all over the USA. [3, 144, 403, 406, 407, 408]

SOLOMON'S PASSAGE c. 1850 Israel Solomon, market gardener. He lived in Pineapple Lodge overlooking Peckham Rye. [180]

SOMERTON ROAD 1892 Site of house called Somerton Lodge. [1, 7, 10]

SOUTH RIDING, 6 Everthorpe Road 1882 (3 Placquett Terrace) Named by Marian and John Beasley when they bought the house in 1972. Marian was born in the South of England (Lewisham) and John at Hornsea in the East Riding of Yorkshire. The house name linked their two birthplaces. After choosing the name they learnt that Winifred Holtby had written a book called *South Riding.* [7, 247, 405]

SOUTHWARK COUNCIL Peckham has been part of the London Borough of Southwark since 1965 when the Metropolitan Boroughs of Bermondsey, Camberwell and Southwark amalgamated. From 1900 Peckham was in the Metropolitan Borough of Camberwell.

The earliest reference to Southwark is in the Burghal Hidage where it is given in the Southern Division as Suthringa Geweorche, a name referring to the defence work of the "Surrey Folke". The Burghal Hidage was a list of burhs with the measure in hides of each territory. It was compiled in 920. [16, 133, 401]

SPIKE, Gordon Road This former workhouse, opened in 1879, was commonly known as "The Spike". The word was first recorded in 1866. In 1906 Bart Kennedy wrote in *Wander Pictures:* "The homeless men who go along the road call the casual ward the spike ... It means that when you have come to the very end of things you are impaled." [210, 213, 214]

SPRINGALL STREET 1875 Mr. Springall who was a builder active locally in the 1870s. [1, 8, 10]

SRI CHINMOY PEACE GARDEN, next to Thomas Calton Centre, Alpha Street Sri Chinmoy is an Indian philosopher, artist and musician whose work aims to promote peace between communities and nations. [412]

STAFFORDSHIRE STREET 1937 (Stafford Street) The Earls of Stafford were Lords of the Manor of Camberwell in the 15th and 16th centuries. [1, 3, 8]

STANBURY ROAD 1877 Possibly John Stanbury (d. 1474), Bishop of Hereford. [1, 6, 7]

STANESGATE HOUSE, Friary Estate 1950 Cluniac nuns community at Stanesgate in Essex. [1, 2, 14, 25, 37]

STANTON STREET 1876 (Royal Place, Cowley Place) Possibly Rev. Dr. Vincent Henry Stanton (1846-1924), Regius Professor of Divinity, University of Cambridge 1916-22. Fellow of Trinity College, 1872. *Trinity in Camberwell: A History of the Trinity College Mission in Camberwell 1885-1985* states: "As Dr. Stanton explained to the College at a meeting on May 18th 1885, 'They applied to the Wilberforce Missioner, Mr. Grundy, and to others, as to parishes which were in need, and went down and saw some which he pointed out to them, and amongst others, St. George's Camberwell. That parish seemed in the greatest need of the kind of work they were to do, and so they selected it'." [7, 202, 348]

STAR OF INDIA, 26 Gordon Road (P) Has as its sign a replica of the medallion of that British order of chivalry known as "The Most Exalted Order of the Star of India". Instituted by Queen Victoria in 1861, as a reward for services in and for India, the motto of the Order is "Heaven's Light our Guide". [294]

STATION COURT, Gibbon Road Close to Nunhead Station. [184]

STATION WAY 1935 (Station Arcade, Railway Approach) Leads to Peckham Rye Station. [8]

STAVELEY CLOSE, Brimmington Estate 1978-80 Staveley in Derbyshire. [2, 5]

STERNHALL LANE Sternhall House, one of the lesser mansions on Peckham Rye. [1, 10]

STOURBRIDGE HOUSE, Sumner Estate 1938 Stourbridge Canal. [1, 2, 69]

STRAKER'S ROAD Straker family who lived in a large house on Peckham Rye called "Sunnyside". Samuel Straker (d. 1874) was a Camberwell Vestryman. [1, 10, 81, 180]

STRICKLAND COURT, East Dulwich Road Estate 1954 Rev. W. J. Strickland, Vicar of St. John's, Goose Green, 1888-1900. [1, 2, 398]

STUART ARMS, 40 Stuart Road (P) See Stuart Road.

STUART ROAD 1901 (Salisbury Villas, Kenilworth Villas, Ledbury Villas, Seymour Villas, Hilda Villas, Malvern Villas, Stuart Villas, Melbourne Cottages) Stuart Villas. [1, 7]

STUDHOLME STREET 1875 Studholme in Cumbria. [1, 4, 7, 25]

STURDY ROAD 1866 Built on land belonging to Daniel Sturdy. [1, 7, 10]

SUMNER ESTATE 1937-54 See Sumner Road. [2]

SUMNER HOUSE (formerly Peckham Manor School) See Sumner Road. [217]

SUMNER NURSERY SCHOOL, Marne House, Sumner Estate Opened in September 1954 and was the first purpose-built nursery school to provide part-time education for London "under fives". See Sumner Road. [359]

SUMNER ROAD 1869 (Willow Brook Road (part), Crab Tree Shot Road, Sumner Street, Charles Street, Sumner Terrace, Winchester Place) Charles Richard Sumner (1790-1874), Bishop of Winchester. [1, 3, 4, 6]

SUNWELL CLOSE, Cossall Estate 1978 Close to former Sunwell Street (1866). [1, 2, 7, 21]

SURE WAY CHRISTIAN CENTRE, Sumner Road Uses a former Primitive Methodist Chapel erected in 1874; Pentecostal since 1921. The present pastor chose Sure Way because Christians believe that following Jesus is the best way to live. [3, 4, 122, 409]

SURREY CANAL LINEAR PARK The Peckham branch of the Grand Surrey Canal was filled in during 1972 and later made into a linear park. The 750th tree was planted early in 1976. [16, 334]

SURREY ROAD 1897 Close to the original boundary between Surrey and Kent. [1, 7]

SURREY VIEW TAVERN, 135-137 Commercial Way (P) Used to overlook Peckham branch of the Grand Surrey Canal. [21, 296]

SWAN, 59 Peckham Park Road (P) In use as a tavern sign since the 14th century, either as a direct allusion to the majestic bird or to a coat of arms which featured it. The sign remains fairly popular, with some thirty examples in Greater London. [295]

SWISS TAVERN, 44 Lausanne Road (P) Name association with Lausanne in Switzerland.

SYLVAN GROVE 1901 Sylvan means "of the woods; having woods; rural" but no record exists of the number of trees planted in the Grove. [1, 19]

SYLVAN TERRACE See Sylvan Grove.

T

TALFOURD PLACE 1884 (Hillsborough Villas, William's Terrace, Denman Cottages) Sir Thomas Noon Talfourd (1795-1854), judge and author. [1, 3, 6, 7]

TALFOURD ROAD 1873 (Hatfield Villas, Pollock Villas, Derby Villas, Rock Terrace, Amesbury Terrace, Alexandra Villas, Surrey Villas, Paradise Villas, Osborne Villas, Pembroke Villas, Melrose Villas) See Talfourd Place. [1,10]

TAMARIND HOUSE, 5 Hereford Retreat 1980 Tamarind – an evergreen tree cultivated in India and other tropical countries. [26, 188]

TAPPESFIELD ESTATE 1964-66 See Tappesfield Road. [2]

TAPPESFIELD ROAD 1877 Henry Tappesfield, 16th century London merchant, married Susan Muschamp of Peckham. [1, 3, 7, 10]

TERN HOUSE, Pelican Estate 1957 Tern. [1, 2, 120]

THAMES COURT, Daniel Gardens 1972 River Thames. [5, 361]

THE GROVE NURSERY SCHOOL See Grove Nursery School.

THOMAS CALTON COMMUNITY EDUCATION CENTRE, Alpha Street (formerly Choumert Road School, 1893) Thomas Calton was a city goldsmith. Henry VIII granted him Dulwich manor in 1545. [3, 159, 160]

THORNBILL HOUSE, 160 Glengall Road 1984 Thornbill, bird belonging to the Hummingbird family. [161, 181]

THORN TERRACE, Nunhead Grove Origin not traced.

THRUXTON WAY, North Peckham Estate 1971 Thruxton in Hampshire. [2, 5]

TILBURY CLOSE, Willowbrook Estate 1963 Tilbury in Essex. [2, 5]

TILLING HOUSE, Nunhead Estate 1950 Thomas Tilling. See *Who Was Who in Peckham*. [1, 2, 17]

TONBRIDGE HOUSE, Willowbrook Estate 1963 Tonbridge in Kent. [2, 5]

TORRIDGE GARDENS, Rye Hill Estate 1958 River Torridge. [1, 2, 92]

TORTINGTON HOUSE, Friary Estate 1950 Austin Canons community at Tortington in West Sussex. [1, 2, 5, 14, 37, 308]

TRAFALGAR, 47 Sumner Road (P) Blanch (1875) refers to national glory in winning the Battle of Trafalgar being represented by "The Trafalgar". [3]

TRAFALGAR AVENUE 1936 (Trafalgar Road) Battle of Trafalgar. A house at the corner of the Old Kent Road, built by John Rolls in 1780, became the Lord Nelson public house after Nelson's death. [1, 8, 10]

TRENT HOUSE, Rye Hill Estate 1938 River Trent. [1, 2, 92]

TRESCO ROAD 1878 Tresco in the Isles of Scilly. [1, 7]

TRINITY COLLEGE CENTRE, 1 Newent Close 1983 Trinity College in Cambridge which started the Trinity College Mission in 1885. [202]

TROY TOWN In 1875 W. H. Blanch wrote in *Ye Parish of Camerwell:* "a small cluster of cottages off Peckham Rye actually bears the imposing title of Troy Town!" Troy Town is a Cornish expression for a labyrinth of streets, a regular maze. [1, 3, 158]

TUKE SCHOOL, 4 Wood's Road 1970 Daniel Hack Tuke (1827-95), a physician who specialised in the field of mental health. [6, 185, 186, 187]

TUSTIN ESTATE 1965 See Tustin Street. [1, 2]

TUSTIN STREET 1874 (Manor Street, York Place) The Tustin family owned and ran a colour and oil works in the road – Jesse Tustin (1814-99) and his sons Charles (1842-1912) and William (1844-93). [1, 7, 180]

TUTSHILL COURT, Gloucester Grove Estate 1975 Tutshill in Gloucestershire. [2, 5]

TYRRELL ARMS, 25 Nunhead Lane (P) 1960s Mary Tyrrell, wife of Sir Claude William Champion de Crespigny. She was the second daughter of Sir John Tyssen Tyrrell, M.P. They married on 22 August 1843. [328, 329, 340]

U

ULLSWATER HOUSE, Tustin Estate Livesey Court, a residential home for elderly people, was converted into a hostel for homeless families in 1992 and renamed Ullswater House. Named after Ullswater in Cumbria. [5, 278, 279, 280]

UNWIN CLOSE 1965 On the site of former Unwin Road (1873) which was probably laid out by Unwins, builders active in South London from c. 1860. [2, 4, 10]

UNWIN ESTATE 1963-65 See Unwin Close. [2]

V

VERVAIN HOUSE, 7 Hereford Retreat 1980 Vervain – a hummingbird. [161, 188]

VICARAGE COURT, Inverton Road Built on the site of St. Silas' Vicarage. [191]

VIVIAN SQUARE, Consort Estate 1978-81 Close to the site of Vivian Road (1876). Sir Richard Hussey (1775-1842), 1st Baron Vivian, married Eliza, daughter of Philip Champion de Crespigny on 14 September 1804. [1, 2, 6, 7, 21, 25]

W

WAGHORN STREET 1876 Before the cutting of the Suez Canal Thomas Waghorn (1800-50) established a reliable overland link between Port Said and Suez as part of a steamer route from Europe to India. Coal was carried by camel train across the desert. [1, 6, 7, 10]

WAGNER STREET 1873 (Cross Street, Coles Buildings) Probably German composer Richard Wagner (1813-83). [1, 7, 26]

WAKEFIELD HOUSE, Oliver Goldsmith Estate 1930 *The Vicar of Wakefield,* a novel by Oliver Goldsmith published in 1766. [1, 2, 23, 93]

WALKFORD WAY, North Peckham Estate 1971 Walkford in Dorset. [2, 5]

WALKYNSCROFT, Brayards Road Estate 1960 A plot of land on the Dulwich Manor. [1, 2, 80]

WALMER CASTLE, 102 Peckham Road (P) Walmer Castle near Deal in Kent. [5]

WARBURTON COURT, East Dulwich Road Estate 1954 Rev. T. A. Warburton, Vicar of St. John's, Goose Green, 1876-88. [1, 2, 82, 398]

WARMLEY COURT, Gloucester Grove Estate 1976 Warmley in Avon. [2, 5]

WARWICK COURT, Choumert Road Possibly Alderman Alfred Warwick. See Warwick Gardens.

WARWICK GARDENS, Lyndhurst Way Alderman Alfred Charles Warwick (?-1951) who was Mayor of Camberwell (1935-36). He first went on to Camberwell Borough Council in 1919. The park was opened in 1963 by the Deputy Mayor of Camberwell, Councillor Edgar Reed, a member of the London County Council for Camberwell. [54, 55, 56, 57]

WARWICK GARDENS HOUSE, 93-99 Azenby Road See Warwick Gardens.

WARWICK PARK SCHOOL, Peckham Road See Warwick Gardens. The school was established in September 1983 by the amalgamation of Peckham, Peckham Manor, Silverthorne and Thomas Calton Schools. The main complex on Peckham Road (formerly Peckham School) was built in 1958 on the site of a mental asylum called Peckham House. [17, 126]

WAVENEY AVENUE 1897 River Waveney. [1, 7, 92]

WAVENEY HOUSE, Rye Hill Estate 1940 See Waveney Avenue. [2]

WAVERLEY ARMS, 202 Ivydale Road (P) On Waverley Park Estate. [4]

WAVERLEY WARD *Waverley,* the first of the novels of Sir Walter Scott, published in 1814. Waverley Park estate was developed by Edward Yates. [4, 23, 367]

WELLAND HOUSE, Rye Hill Estate 1938 River Welland. [1, 2, 92]

WENTWORTH CRESCENT, Bells Gardens Estate 1980 All the blocks of flats on this estate were said to be named after characters in Oliver Goldsmith's works. Wentworth is not in the index to the *Collected Works of Oliver Goldsmith.* [2, 93, 400]

WESTONBIRT COURT, Gloucester Grove Estate 1976 Westonbirt in Gloucestershire. [2, 5]

WHITE HORSE, 20 Peckham Rye (P) 1930s This sign has been in use since the 15th century and remains very frequent because of its widespread heraldic usage. A galloping white horse refers heraldically to the House of Hanover, and dates from the accession of George I in 1714. [295, 340]

WHITMINSTER COURT, Gloucester Grove Estate 1978 Whitminster in Gloucestershire. [2, 5]

WHITTEN TIMBER LTD., Eagle Wharf, Peckham Hill Street (B) The founder of the business was Mr. W. H. Whitten who commenced trading in 1919 from his home by selling secondhand timber, doors, windows, etc. from London County Council schools that were being replaced by more modern buildings. His business prospered and in 1921 he moved to Canal Head to begin trading in softwoods. [164]

WHORLTON ROAD 1888 Probably Whorlton in North Yorkshire. [1, 5, 7]

W. H. SMITH, The Aylesham Centre, Rye Lane (B) William Henry Smith (1792-1865), son of the firm's founder, Henry Walton Smith who established a tiny "newswalk" in 1792 in Little Grosvenor Street, London. [316, 317]

WICKWAY COURT, Gloucester Grove Estate 1976 Wickwar (sic.) in Avon. [2, 5]

WILKINSON HOUSE, Dewar Street Sir George Wilkinson (1885-1967), Lord Mayor of London (1940-41). He was the first chairman of the London Homes for the Elderly. The foundation stone was laid by Sir Dennis Truscott in 1957 and the building was completed in 1958. It was opened by Her Majesty, Queen Elizabeth, The Queen Mother. [50, 51, 52, 53]

WILLIAM MARGRIE CLOSE, Moncrieff Estate 1978 William Margrie. See *Who Was Who in Peckham.* [2, 17]

WILLOWBROOK ESTATE 1962-76 See Willowbrook Road. [2]

WILLOWBROOK ROAD 1892 (Birkbeck Place, Bangor Crescent, Willowbrook Terrace, Amelia Terrace, Elizabeth Terrace) It is believed there was a brook nearby at one time. Withee Brook Field is shown on a 1739 map. A field name in the Trevor/Hill/Shard estate was Withey Brooke Shott. [1, 7, 198, 410]

WILLOWBROOK URBAN STUDIES CENTRE See Willowbrook Road. Opened on 2 November 1985 by Coun. Geoff Williams, Chair of Southwark Council's Planning Committee. [245]

WILLOWDENE, Acorn Estate 1962 Willow tree. Dene means vale. [1, 2, 19]

WILLSBRIDGE COURT, Gloucester Grove Estate 1976 Willsbridge in Avon. [2, 5]

WILMOT CLOSE, Bells Gardens Estate 1980 Miss Arabella Wilmot in *The Vicar of Wakefield* by Oliver Goldsmith. [2, 93, 400]

WINCHCOMBE BUSINESS CENTRE (B) 1989 See Winchcombe Court. [192]

WINCHCOMBE COURT, Gloucester Grove Estate 1976 Winchcombe in Gloucestershire. [2, 5]

WINDERMERE POINT, Tustin Estate 1965 Windermere in Cumbria. [2, 5]

WINDSOR COURT, Chadwick Road 1987 Extracted at random from the Outer London telephone directory. [201]

WINDSPOINT DRIVE, Ledbury Estate 1969 Wynds Point in Hereford and Worcester. [2, 283]

WINGFIELD MEWS See Wingfield Street.

WINGFIELD STREET 1876 (Hadfield Terrace, Whittington Terrace) Wingfield in Derbyshire. Hadfield and Whittington are both in Derbyshire. [1, 7]

WINNIE MANDELA HOUSE, Peckham Road (formerly Pelican House) Anti-apartheid campaigner Winnie Mandela. [141, 149, 150, 151, 152, 156, 305]

WISHING WELL INN, 77-79 Choumert Road (P) Named by the proprietor Mike McCann after the wishing well at Kingscourt, County Cavan, Ireland. Mr. McCann was born in that county. [268]

WITCOMBE POINT, Clifton Estate 1970 Great Witcombe in Gloucestershire. [2, 5]

WITHINGTON COURT, Gloucester Grove Estate 1977 Withington in Gloucestershire. [2, 5]

WIVENHOE CLOSE 1979 Wivenhoe Hall in Essex, the home of Sir Claude William Champion de Crespigny. [10, 329, 361]

WOOD DENE, Acorn Estate 1963 The flats on this estate are associated with trees. See Acorn Estate. [2]

WOODS ROAD 1866 (Edward Terrace) Charles Wood, landowner in c. 1830. [1, 7, 10]

WOODSTAR HOUSE, 6 Hereford Retreat 1980 Woodstar – a hummingbird. [161, 188]

WOODSTOCK SCHOOL, Adys Road When the school was opened in April 1963, it was in premises in Marlborough Road and so the name Marlborough was considered. As this name had already been used, the name Woodstock was chosen as having an association with Marlborough. (See Blenheim Grove.) Woodstock School moved to Ruby Street in June 1966. In 1979 the school moved temporarily to Camberwell. The school then moved to Adys Road in September 1985. It took over what latterly had been Thomas Calton Lower School. [197]

WOOLWORTHS, Rye Lane (B) Frank Winfield Woolworth (1852-1919). An American entrepreneur who with his brother C. S. Woolworth (1856-1947) built up a chain of shops. [227]

WROXTON ROAD 1877 Wroxton in Oxfordshire. [1, 5, 7]

YARNFIELD SQUARE, Clifton Estate 1970 Yarnfield in Wiltshire, transferred from Somerset in 1895. [2, 199, 200]

YORK GROVE 1898 George, who was created Duke of York in 1892. He became King George V in 1910. [1, 7, 26]

KEY TO SOURCES AND FURTHER READING

1. *Camberwell Place and Street Names and their Origin* by L. S. Sherwood. Camberwell Borough Council, 1964.
2. List of property owned by Southwark Council administered by the Camberwell, Dulwich and Peckham housing offices, 1987.
3. *Ye Parish of Camerwell* by W. H. Blanch. E. W. Allen, 1875.
4. *Victorian Suburb* by H. J. Dyos. Leicester University Press, 1966.
5. *Bartholomew Gazetteer of Places in Britain* compiled by Oliver Mason. John Bartholomew, 1986.
6. *Dictionary of National Biography.*
7. *List of the Streets and Places within the Administrative County of London.* London County Council, 1929.
8. *Names of Streets and Places in the Administrative County of London.* London County Council, 1955.
9. *The Gazetteer of England* by Oliver Mason. David & Charles, 1972.
10. *The Streets of London: A dictionary of the names and their origins* by S. Fairfield. Papermac, 1983.
11. *The Buildings of England LONDON 2: SOUTH* by Bridget Cherry and Nikolaus Pevsner. Penguin, 1983.
12. Property Brochure Camberwell District J. O'Brien January 1982.
13. Property Brochure Dulwich District J. O'Brien January 1982.
14. Property Brochure Peckham District J. O'Brien November 1982.
15. North Peckham Project. London Borough of Southwark. (S.C. P711. 5 NOR).
16. *The Story of Peckham* by John D. Beasley. London Borough of Southwark, 1983.
17. *Who Was Who in Peckham* by John D. Beasley. Chener Books, 1985.
18. *The Canals of South Wales and the Border* by Charles Hadfield. David & Charles, 1967.
19. *The Concise Oxford Dictionary* edited by J. B. Sykes. Oxford University Press, 1983.
20. Old Ordnance Survey Maps: Old Kent Road 1914. The Godfrey Edition.
21. Old Ordnance Survey Maps: Peckham 1914. The Godfrey Edition.
22. *The Place-Names of Dorset* by A. D. Mills. English Place-Name Society, 1980.
23. *The Oxford Companion to English Literature* edited by Margaret Drabble. Oxford University Press, 1985.
24. *The Canals of South and South East England* by Charles Hadfield. David & Charles, 1969.
25. *Office of Population Censuses and Surveys Census 1981 Index of Place Names.* H.M.S.O., 1985.
26. *Everyman's Encyclopaedia* edited by D. A. Girling. J. M. Dent, 1978.
27. *Gazetteer of Scotland* revised by R. W. Munro. Johnston and Bacon, 1973.
28. The Girdlers Company.
29. *Who's Who in Shakespeare* by Peter Quennell and Hamish Johnson. Weidenfeld and Nicolson, 1973.

30. *The Canals of South Wales and The Border* by Charles Hadfield. David & Charles, 1967.
31. *The Canals of South West England* by Charles Hadfield. David & Charles, 1985.
32. *Who Was Who 1897-1916.* Adam & Charles Black, 1967.
33. *South London Press* 31 January 1986 – Letter from Coun. Tony Goss.
34. Peckham Society Newsletter Spring 1986.
35. *Looking Back: Photographs of Camberwell and Peckham 1860-1918.* Peckham Publishing Project, 1979.
36. *Acorn wharf 1855-1955: The Story of R. May & Son Limited.* R. May & Son Ltd., 1955.
37. *English Monastic Life* by Abbot Gasquet. Methuen, 1904.
38. Plaque inside Ammon.
39. *Who Was Who 1951-1960.* Adam & Charles Black, 1961.
40. *The New Century Cyclopedia of Names* edited by Clarence L. Barnhart. Prentice-Hall, 1954.
41. *The Peckham Society News* Spring 1993.
42. *British Canals: An Illustrated History* by Charles Hadfield. David & Charles, 1984.
43. *Building Together: The Story of Peckham Methodist Church* by John D. Beasley. Peckham Methodist Church, 1985.
44. *Centenary Viewpoint St. Antony's Nunhead 1878-1978* edited by Roger Smith. St. Antony's Church, Nunhead, 1978.
45. *"I Think of My Mother" Notes on the Life and Times of Claudia Jones* by Buzz Johnson. Karia Press, 1985.
46. *South London Record* No. 2 1987. South London History Workshop, 1987.
47. *Burke's Peerage, Baronetage, Knightage 1897.* Harrison, 1897.
48. *Armorial Families: A Directory of Gentlemen of Coat-Armour* compiled and edited by Arthur Charles Fox-Davies. Hurst and Blackett, 1929.
49. *Southwark Civic News* July 1969.
50. London Homes for the Elderly (pamphlet).
51. *The Daily Telegraph* 27 August 1962.
52. *South London Press* 24 September 1974.
53. *Who Was Who 1961-1970.* Adam & Charles Black, 1972.
54. *South London Observer* 26 April 1951.
55. *South London Observer* 16 July 1959.
56. *South London Press* 8 November 1963.
57. *Metropolitan Borough of Camberwell Twenty-Second Report of the Council from 1st April 1935 to 31st March 1936.*
58. *Southwark Civic News* July 1971.
59. *The Times* 4 April 1960.
60. Southwark Collection Calendar of Deeds.
61. *The Victoria History of the Counties of England: Surrey* edited by H E Malden Constable, 1912.

62. *Retracing Canals to Croydon and Camberwell.* Living History Publications and Environment Bromley, 1986.

63. *South London Press* 19 August 1983.

64. *The New Encyclopaedia Britannica.* 1986.

65. *Palace of the People* by Graham Reeves. Bromley Library Service, 1986.

66. *Burke's Peerage* edited by Peter Townend. Burke's Peerage, 1963.

67. *Hanover Chapel (Congregational) Bellenden Road, Peckham, London, SE15 celebrates 300 years of Christian witness.* 1957.

68. *A Shell Guide: Staffordshire* by Henry Thorold. Faber and Faber, 1978.

69. *The Canals of the West Midlands* by Charles Hadfield. David & Charles, 1985.

70. *The King's England The Lake District Cumberland Westmorland* by Arthur Mee. Hodder and Stoughton, 1967.

71. *Joseph Lister* by Richard B. Fisher. Stein and Day, 1977.

72. *King's College Hospital Gazette* February 1978.

73. *The Story of King's College Hospital* by David Jenkins and Andrew T. Stanway. King's College Hospital, 1968.

74. *South London Press* 7 February 1978.

75. *Stately Homes, Museums, Castles and Gardens in Britain 1987* edited by Penny Hicks. Automobile Association, 1986.

76. *Islington Elfrida Rathbone Association Annual Report 1986/87.*

77. *The Canals of North West England* (volume 1) by Charles Hadfield and Gordon Biddle. David & Charles, 1970.

78. *St. Giles, Camberwell, Surrey Eleventh Annual Report of the Vestry 1867.*

79. The Copleston Centre.

80. *The History of Dulwich College* by William Young. 1889.

81. *St. Giles, Camberwell, Surrey Seventh Annual Report of the Vestry 1863.*

82. List of vicars of St. John's, Goose Green, supplied by Mary Boast.

83. Letter from The Tilt Estate Co. dated 17 November 1987.

84. *South London Observer* 4 August 1960.

85. Letter dated 19 November 1987 from Mrs. Margaret Bruce, daughter of Arnold Dobson.

86. Obituary of Arnold Dobson in *Contact* (published by Dulwich Labour Party), 1980.

87. *South London Advertiser* 5 April 1974.

88. Extract from an article in Southwark Local Studies Library (PC 929.4B) written by W.J.A. Hahn.

89. Undated letter in Southwark Local Studies Library from W.J.A. Hahn (Chief Librarian, Camberwell Public Libraries) – PC 929.4.

90. *Everyman's Dictionary of Fictional Characters* by William Freeman. J.M. Dent, 1973.

91. *Who's Who of British Members of Parliament* (Volume IV 1945-1979) edited by M. Stenton and S. Lees. Harvester Press, 1981.

92. *English River-Names* by Eilert Ekwall. Oxford, 1928.

93. *Collected Works of Oliver Goldsmith* ed. by Arthur Friedman. Oxford, 1966.

94. *The Oxford Companion to Classical Literature* compiled and edited by Sir Paul Harvey. Oxford, 1974.
95. *Who's Who 1987.* A & C Black, 1987.
96. *St. Giles, Camberwell, Surrey, Nineteenth Annual Report of the Vestry 1874-75.*
97. *Southwark Civic News* July 1979.
98. *South London Press* 3 September 1982.
99. *South London Press* 17 August 1984.
100. *Cyclopedia of Classified Dates* by Charles E. Little. Funk and Wagnalls, 1900.
101. *St. Luke's Lads' Club.* pub. 1912.
102. *A Tour of Camberwell* by Olive M. Walker. H. H. Greaves, 1954.
103. *South London Press* 31 May 1985.
104. *The Inquirer* 25 April 1885.
105. *The Inquirer* 2 May 1885.
106. *Camden Parish Magazine* April 1892 (p. 61).
107. Minutes of meeting of trustees of Camden Chapel held on 17 June 1796.
108. *The Canals of Yorkshire and North East England* (Volume 1) by Charles Hadfield. David & Charles, 1972.
109. *Southwark Sparrow* September 1987.
110. *South London Press* 30 June 1987.
111. *News on Sunday* 5 July 1987.
112. *Labour Weekly* 10 July 1987.
113. *T & G Record* August 1987.
114. *Bellenden News* August/September 1987.
115. *South London Press* 14 July 1987.
116. Letter from Jack Jones to the author dated 11 July 1987.
117. *Southwark Civic News* March 1981.
118. *Kentish Mercury* 19 December 1958.
119. *The Parks and Woodlands of London* by Andrew Crowe. Fourth Estate, 1987.
120. *A Dictionary of Birds* ed. by Bruce Campbell and Elizabeth Lack. T. & A. D. Poyser, 1985.
121. *Shorter Oxford Dictionary.* Clarendon Press, 1977.
122. *London South of the Thames* by Sir Walter Besant. Adam & Charles Black, 1912.
123. Letter dated 23 March 1988 from Margaret Sawyers, Co-ordinator, Black Elderly Group Southwark.
124. Social and Economic Effects on Gloucester Road Primary School by Pamela Knowler, 1970.
125. *A view of Dulwich, Peckham and Camberwell around 1300* by R.J. Warhurst, 1985.
126. South West Quadrant Review Facts and Figures. ILEA.
127. *The Westminster Dictionary of the Bible* by John D. Davis. Collins' Clear-Type Press, 1944.
128 *1863-64 St. Giles, Camberwell, Surrey Eighth Annual Report of the Vestry.*

129. *The Orchard Mission's 50th Annual Report,* 1937.
130. *St. Giles: The Parish Church of Camberwell* by Mary Boast. Friends of St. Giles Church, 1987.
131. *Nelson's War* by Peter Padfield. Hart-Davis, MacGibbon, 1976.
132. *Imperial Dictionary of Universal Biography* edited by John Francis Waller. William Mackenzie 1857-63.
133. *The Concise Oxford Dictionary of English Place-Names* by Eilert Ekwall. Oxford, 1974.
134. Metropolitan Borough of Camberwell Official Guide. Ninth edition, 1955.
135. *G. W. Marsden: A Memoir* by Edward Foskett. Privately printed, 1896.
136. *A Dictionary of Rhyming Slang* by Julian Franklyn. Routledge & Kegan Paul, 1975.
137. Deed 9380 – Southwark Local Studies Library.
138. *The Forgotten Stations of Greater London* by J.E. Connor and B.L. Halford. Forge Books, 1978.
139. *Nunhead Notables* by Ron Woollacott. Friends of Nunhead Cemetery, 1984.
140. *Roman Ways in the Weald* by Ivan D. Margary. Phoenix House, 1965.
141. *Nelson Mandela* by Mary Benson. Penguin, 1986.
142. *Methodism* by Rupert E. Davies. Epworth Press, 1963.
143. Map of the Parish of St. Giles Camberwell, delineating its ecclesiastical and parochial districts, 1842. By J. Dewhirst, civil engineer.
144. *The Architecture of Peckham* by Tim Charlesworth. Chener Books, 1988.
145. *Nunhead Cemetery: An Illustrated Guide.* Friends of Nunhead Cemetery, 1988.
146. *Old Surviving Firms of South London* by Steven Harris. 1987.
147. St. Mary Magdalene, Peckham – brochure prepared for opening of church consecrated on 3 November 1962.
148. Supplement to the Camberwell Society Newsletter No. 38 July 1977.
149. *South London Press* 24 January 1989.
150. *Deptford and Peckham Mercury* 26 January 1989.
151. *Governing London* 26 January 1989.
152. *Dulwich, Peckham and Walworth Comet* 1 February 1989.
153. *Southwark Sparrow* 6 February 1989.
154. *Kelly's London Suburban Directory 1884.*
155. Ordnance Survey Map (1st edition).
156. *Winnie Mandela: Part of My Soul* by Anne Benjamin. Penguin, 1985.
157. *Robert Browning and His World: The Private Face (1812-1861)* by Maisie Ward. Cassell, 1968.
158. *Brewer's Dictionary of Phrase and Fable* by Ivor H. Evans. Cassell, 1983.
159. *The Great North Wood: A brief history of ancient woodlands from Selhurst to Deptford* by L.S.C. Neville. London Wildlife Trust, Southwark Group, 1987.
160. *Dulwich Discovered* by William Darby. Published by the author, 1974.
161. *Finding Birds Around the World* by Peter Alden and John Gooders. Andre Deutsch, 1981.

162. *Every Man's Book of Saints* by C.P.S. Clarke. A.R. Mowbray, 1948.

163. Letter dated 17 April 1989 from Mrs. Kate McGuinness, Headteacher, St. Alban's R.C. Primary School.

164. *Timber Trades Journal* 12 February 1977.

165. Letter dated 29 June 1987 from A.C.L. Hall, Librarian, Dulwich College.

166. *Daily Chronicle* 4 September 1926.

167. *South London Observer* 30 December 1954.

168. *The Oxford Encyclopedia of Trees of the World.* Consultant Editor: Bayard Hora. Oxford University Press, 1981.

169. *Berkshire* by Ian Yarrow. Robert Hale, 1974.

170. Letter dated 20 June 1989 from John McNicol, Managing Director, Groveside Homes, 89-91 Hartfield Road, Wimbledon, SW19 3TJ.

171. Letter dated 23 June 1989 from D.J. Forge, Area Housing Manager, Church Housing Association.

172. *Supplement to Names of Streets and Places in the Former Administrative County of London for 1955-1966.* Greater London Council, 1967.

173. *Lockerbie and its Story: the town's history – and other articles* by Rev. John C. Steen, n.d.

174. Letter dated 16 March 1989 from Mrs. Nancy Hammond, Southwark Personnel and Management Services, John Carter House, 25 Commercial Way, SE15 6DG.

175. *Medieval Religious Houses in Scotland* by Ian B. Cowan and David E. Easson. Longman, 1976.

176. *The Story of the London Boroughs: Camberwell.* E. J. Burrows, ?1936.

177. *The Canals of South West England* by Charles Hadfield. David & Charles, 1985.

178. *Kelly's London Suburban Directory 1888 Southern Suburbs.*

179. *The New Shell Guide to Scotland* edited by Donald Lamond Macnie and Moray McLaren. Ebury Press, 1977.

180. Street names in Nunhead: list compiled by Ron Woollacott. 1989.

181. Old Ordnance Survey Maps. East Dulwich and Peckham Rye, 1914. Godfrey Edition.

182. *1871-72 St. Giles Camberwell Surrey Sixteenth Annual Report of the Vestry.*

183. *Encyclopaedia Britannica,* 1951.

184. Author's observations.

185. Letter from Miss P. Davy, headmistress, Tuke School dated 8 August 1986.

186. *Southwark Civic News* October 1970.

187. Tuke Junior Training School SLSL 371.92.

188. Letter dated 21 March 1989 from Joan Khachik, Estate Office, Hyde Housing Association.

189. *Old Ordnance Survey Maps Brockley 1868.* Alan Godfrey Maps.

190. Map of an estate situate at or near Peckham in the Parish of St. Giles Camberwell and County of Surrey. The freehold property of Charles Shard Esq. Surveyed April 1831.

191. Ordnance Survey Map. 1914.

192. *South London Press* 8 December 1989.
193. Letter from the Bishop of Croydon dated 8 January 1990.
194. Letter from the Bishop of Croydon to the African Refugee Housing Action Ltd. dated 20 October 1989.
195. Press release from ARHAG Housing Association Ltd. dated 6 December 1989.
196. *Who's Who 1989.* A. & C. Black, 1989.
197. Letter dated 9 July 1987 from Mr. M. J. Gavin, headmaster, Woodstock School
198. A Survey of the whole Manor of Frerne, and part of the Manor of Buckingham and Kenninton, in the Parish of Camberwell the Estate of Joseph Windham Ash Esq. taken in 1739.
199. Letter dated 10 April 1990 from David Bromwich, Local History Librarian, Somerset County Council.
200. Letter dated 10 June 1966 from Hubert Bennett, Superintending Architect of Metropolitan Buildings, Greater London Council.
201. Notes provided in 1990 by Mrs. Joy Broadbent, Engineering and Public Works Department, Southwark Council.
202. *Trinity in Camberwell: A History of the Trinity College Mission in Camberwell 1885-1985* by Lawrence Goldman. Trinity College Cambridge, 1985.
203. *Southwark a London Borough* by Mary Boast. Southwark Council, 1975.
204. Minutes of Proceedings of the Metropolitan Board of Works 1869.
205. Proceedings of the Royal Society Volume 82, 1909.
206. Monthly Notice of the Royal Astronomical Society Volume 69, 1909.
207. *The Story of Dulwich* by Mary Boast. London Borough of Southwark, 1990.
208. Southwark Engineering and Public Works: Numbering of Buildings notice dated 29 January 1987.
209. Letter dated 30 May 1990 from Margaret Reynolds, Sales Supervisor, Balfour Beatty Homes, Leatherhead, Surrey.
210. *The Oxford English Dictionary* Second Edition. Prepared by J.A. Simpson and E.S.C. Weiner. Clarendon Press, 1989.
211. *St. Saviour's Parish News* November 1977.
212. Plan of the South Common Fields, Peckham, Surrey 1830.
213. *A Dictionary of the Underworld* by Eric Partridge. Routledge & Kegan Paul, 1968.
214. Date on the workhouse in Gordon Road which became Camberwell Reception Centre and later Camberwell Resettlement Unit.
215. Letter dated 23 November 1990 from M. Baker, Southwark Engineering and Public Works Department.
216. *Nature Conservation in Southwark* by John Archer et al. London Ecology Unit, 1989.
217. Adult Education Southwark 1990/91.
218. Letter dated 29 November 1990 from R. W. Standley, Chairman, Newgate Press Ltd., Colour Lithographers.
219. Chambers World Gazetteer edited by David Munro. Chambers, 1988.
220. Letter dated 22 November 1990 from R. A. Roffey, Archivist, Co-operative Wholesale Society Ltd.

221. Information obtained by telephone on 19 December 1990 from a member of staff of Mother Goose Nursery.

222. *The Local* 11 December 1990.

223. Plaque inside Helena Day Nursery.

224. *South London Press* 21 December 1990

225. Letter dated 3 January 1991 from Karen Ody, Comet Group plc.

226. *South London Press* 27 November 1987.

227. *The Hutchinson Paperback Dictionary of Biography* edited by Michael Upshall. Arrow Books, 1990.

228. Letter dated 27 December 1990 from Brian M. Jay.

229. Letter dated 19 February 1976 from A.W. Whitehead (Director), Parma Agency Ltd.

230. *The History of St. John (Chrysostom) with St. Andrew, Peckham* by Leslie Mole.

231. *The Penguin Dictionary of Saints* by Donald Attwater. Penguin, 1983.

232. Tithe Map and Camberwell Schedules, 1837. Tithe Commissioners.

233. *South London Observer* 9 March 1961.

234. *South London Press* 17 June 1977.

235. Letter dated 28 March 1991 from M. Baker, Head of Support Services, for Director of Engineering and Public Works, London Borough of Southwark.

236. London County Council Minutes of Proceedings July-December, 1931.

237. *Southwark Sparrow* 16 August 1991.

238. Letter dated 17 October 1991 from Leah Leisurewear.

239. Information provided by Argos Distributors Limited.

240. *South London Press* 21 January 1992.

241. B & Q Brochure.

242. *Church Army Review* June 1933.

243. *South London Observer* 13 May 1933.

244. *South London Press* 12 May 1933.

245. Letter from Judy Woodman, Chair of Management Committee of Willowbrook Urban Studies Centre dated 14 October 1985.

246. Argos New Store Openlng Peckham.

247. *South Riding* by Winifred Holtby. William Collins, 1936.

248. Letter from St. James' Catholic Church dated 1 March 1976.

249. *The Oxford Book of Saints* by David Hugh Farmer. Oxford University Press, 1987.

250. *South London Press* 16 September 1988.

251. Note from Robin Thomas, Managing Director, Abbey Rose & Co. Ltd. received in February 1992.

252. Minutes of Proceedings of the Metropolitan Board of Works 1863.

253. *Post Office London Directory 1892 Volume 2 Trades and Professional.*

254. *Camberwell and Neighbourhood* by Douglas Allport. 1841.

255. *1888-89 St. Giles Camberwell Surrey Thirty-Third Annual Report of the Vestry*

256. *South London Press* 24 November 1987.

257. *South London Press* 3 March 1992.

258. *A Latin Dictionary* by Charlton T. Lewis & Charles Short. Oxford University Press, 1966.

259. *JS 100 The Story of Sainsbury's* edited by James Boswell. J. Sainsbury, 1969.

260. *Daily Mail* 25 November 1982.

261. Photograph from an unnamed and undated magazine with caption – *50 years on – Peckham's Rye Lane branch on its opening day on November 6, 1931.*

262. *JS Journal* September 1983.

263. *The first 120 years of Sainsbury's 1869-1989.*

264. *St. Mary Magdalene Magazine* June 1906.

265. *St. Mary Magdalene Peckham Parish Church Magazine Centenary Number 1841-1941* May 1941.

266. Letter from the Rev. C. L. Green dated 25 March 1992.

267. The Latter-Rain Outpouring Revival Constitution & Beliefs.

268. Information provided by Mike McCann on 31 March 1992.

269. Notes in Southwark Local Studies Library.

270. Borough of Camberwell Minutes of Proceedings of Council Volume 62 (May 1962-April 1963).

271. Letter from L. C. Pollard dated 18 April 1992.

272. *South London Press* 13 March 1992.

273. *Newham/Docklands Recorder* 23 January 1992.

274. Information provided on 28 April 1992 by Mrs. Mary Beattie.

275. Information provided on 28 April 1992 by Mrs. Stewart-Paver.

276. Halfords New Superstore Opens this Saturday in the Old Kent Road!

277. Letter dated 24 June 1992 from David Warburton, Marketing Executive, Halfords.

278. *Southwark and Bermondsey News* 16 July 1992.

279. *South London Press* 17 July 1992.

280. *Southwark Sparrow* 17 July 1992.

281. *South London Press* 3 July 1992.

282. *Southwark and Bermondsey News* 1 July 1992.

283. Ordnance Survey Landranger Gazetteer on microfiche, 1989.

284. *The Oxford Dictionary of the Christian Church* edited by F. L. Cross. Oxford University Press, 1963.

285. *East Dulwich Baptist Church: An abridged history of the Church.* 1973.

286. *Christ Church Evangelical Free Church 1880-1980.*

287. *St. Mary Magdalene, Peckham.*

288. *100 Years of Service!* Peckham Park Road Baptist Chapel, 1953.

289. *Nunhead Cemetery, London: A History of the Planning, Architecture, Landscaping and Fortunes of a Great Nineteenth-century Cemetery by James Stevens Curl.*

290. *Who's Who 1992.* A & C Black, 1992.

291. *Ghosts of London* by Jack Hallan. Wolfe, 1975.

292. *The Architects' Journal* 30 May 1957.
293. Letter dated 17 February 1954 from the Chief Librarian and Curator for Camberwell.
294. *Stories of Inns and Their Signs* by Eric R. Delderfield. David & Charles, 1974.
295. *A Dictionary of Pub Names* by Leslie Dunkling and Gordon Wright. Routledge & Kegan Paul, 1987.
296. Cassell's Map of the Suburbs of London, 1870.
297. *Inns and their Signs: Fact and Fiction* by Eric R. Delderfield. David & Charles, 1975.
298. Pub sign.
299. Centenary of the Capuchin Franciscan Church of our Lady of Seven Dolours, 1966.
300. *A Catholic Dictionary* by William E. Addis et al. Routledge & Kegan Paul, 1960.
301. Plaque in The Aylesham Centre.
302. *Peckham Park Schools* edited by Vera K. A. Conway. Peckham Park School, 1989.
303. *English Inn Signs* by Jacob Larwood and John Camden Hotten. Blaketon Hall, 1985.
304. *Nunhead Resident* Issue no. 10.
305. *Winnie Mandela: Mother of a Nation* by Nancy Harrison. Victor Gollancz, 1985.
306. *Elizabeth Tudor: Portrait of a Queen* by Lacey Baldwin Smith. Hutchinson, 1976.
307. Information obtained from an employee of McCabe's Tavern on 21 October 1992.
308. *English Medieval Monasteries 1066-1540* by Roy Midmer. Heinemann, 1979.
309. Pictorial display on the history of St. Luke's Church deposited in Southwark Local Studies Library.
310. *A key to the door: the Abbey National story* by Berry Ritchie. Abbey National, 1990.
311. Note from Erica Harper, Press Office, Abbey National plc, in October 1992.
312. *Life and Labour of the People in London* by Charles Booth. (Third Series: Religious Influences. Outer South London.) Macmillan, 1902.
313. Information obtained from Bishop B. A. Pitt on 5 September and 28 October 1992.
314. Memorial inside Highshore School.
315. Information obtained in October 1992 by Heather Cragg from a resident of Brookstone Court who moved there a few months after it opened. Building work began in 1938 and finished in 1940.
316. *First with the News: The History of W. H. Smith 1792-1972* by Charles Wilson. Jonathan Cape, 1985.
317. *New Technology New Markets: W. H. Smith through Two Centuries* Designed by Carroll, Dempsey and Thirkell. W. H. Smith Group PLC, 1992.
318. Dr. Iain Stevenson in *The Guardian* on 1 July 1991.
319. *Southwark Civic News* January 1976.
320. Map of London Borough of Southwark: Proposed Wards 1978.
321. *Kelly's London Suburban Directory for 1896.*
322. Information held on microfiche by Southwark Planning.
323. *Collins English Dictionary* edited by Patrick Hanks. Collins, 1986.
324. *The London Encyclopaedia* edited by Ben Weinreb and Christopher Hibbert Papermac, 1988.
325. *The Times Index-Gazetteer of the World.* Times Publishing, 1965.

326. *The Mercury* 26 March 1986.
327. Information provided in November 1992 by Mr. Mence of Peckham Rye Tabernacle Baptist Church.
328. *Complete Baronetage* edited by George Edward Cokayne. Alan Sutton, 1983.
329. *A Genealogical and Heraldic Dictionary of the Peerage and Baronetage of the British Empire* by Sir Bernard Burke. Harrison, 1868.
330. *The Gentleman's Magazine* September 1761.
331. *The London Magazine* August 1761.
332. *Obituary prior to 1800* compiled by Sir William Musgrave. Harleian Society, 1899-1901.
333. Letter dated 13 November 1992 from Colin Brand, Park Services Manager, Southwark Council.
334. *South London Press* 6 February 1976.
335. *The Street Names of England* by Adrian Room. Paul Watkins, 1992.
336. *Peckham Rye Park 1894-1994* by John D. Beasley. To be published on 14 May 1994 by South Riding Press.
337. Letter dated 24 November 1992 from Ord, Carmell & Kritzler.
338. *The Honor Oak School Golden Jubilee 1906-1956.*
339. Information obtained from a local resident.
340. *A Historical Tour of Nunhead and Peckham Rye* by Ron Woollacott. Special Limited Edition produced by the author, 1992.
341. *London Inns and Taverns* by Leopold Wagner. George Allen & Unwin, 1924.
342. *The Wonderful Story of London* edited by Harold Wheeler. Odhams Press, 1937.
343. Information obtained on 2 December 1992 from Mrs. Anderson of Leah Leisurewear.
344. Letter dated 27 November 1992 from Carol Harrison, Environmental Services Department, Southwark Council.
345. Memo dated 30 November 1992 from David Solman, Development Department, Southwark Council.
346. Celestial Church of Christ Constitution.
347. *Divine Spiritual Message* by Rev. Pastor Founder and Prophet S.B.J. Oshoffa.
348. *Who Was Who 1916-1928.* Adam & Charles Black, 1967.
349. *The Builder* 24 September 1881.
350. Notes on Waverley Park Estate written by Ron Woollacott who suggests that the names are probably romantic compositions. None appears elsewhere in London.
351. *The Story of Congregationalism in Surrey* by Edward E. Cleal. James Clarke, 1908.
352. *The Baptist Churches of Surrey* edited by Arthur H. Stockwell. Stockwell, c. 1910.
353. *A Cure of Delinquents: The Treatment of Maladjustment* by Robert W. Shields. Heinemann, 1962.
354. *The Mercury* 8 August 1985.
355. De Laune Gazette No. 1 Vol. 1 (22 November 1894).
356. *A Century Awheel 1889-1989: A History of the De Laune Cycling Club* by Mike Rabbetts.
357. *The Catholic Directory of England and Wales 1992.* Gabriel Communications Ltd., 1992.

358. Information obtained on 17 December 1992 from Joan Bond, former librarian of St. Thomas the Apostle School.

359. Letter dated 20 October 1977 from Miss G. M. Cronin, Headmistress, Sumner Nursery School.

360. Information obtained in 1977 from the headmaster of Bredinghurst School.

361. Computer print-out of properties in SE15 managed by Southwark Council (1993). Some dates are slightly different from those recorded in [2].

362. *Achievement: A short history of the London County Council* by W. Eric Jackson. Longmans, 1965.

363. *Regiments and Corps of the British Army* by Ian S. Hallows. Arms & Armour Press, 1991.

364. Foundation stone at Howard Court.

365. *South London Press* 25 March 1938.

366. Notes provided on 21 October 1977 by A. G. Larter, Headmaster, The Highshore School.

367. *Exploring the Urban Past: Essays in urban history by H. J. Dyos* edited by David Cannadine and David Reeder. Cambridge University Press, 1982.

368. *Anglo-Saxon England 2* edited by Peter Clemoes. Cambridge University Press, 1973.

369. *The Place-Names of Surrey* edited by A. Mawer and F. M. Stenton. Cambridge University Press, 1934.

370. *Gazetteer of the British Isles.* John Bartholomew, 1971.

371. Letter dated 4 January 1993 from Robert F. Tennant, Divisional Organiser, Reference and Information Services, North Yorkshire County Council.

372. ILEA letter dated 6 February 1968 in the possession of Pilgrim's Way School.

373. *Evening News and Star* 27 May 1968.

374. *Evening News and Star* 30 May 1968.

375. Information provided on 6 January 1993 by Esther Hothersall, Head, The Grove Nursery School.

376. *ILEA Contact* 28 February 1975.

377. Information provided on 9 January 1993 by Lisa Evans, a resident of Laburnum Close.

378. *The Mercury* 27 March 1969.

379. Information on the history of Pilgrim's Way School provided on 7 January 1993 by Dave Boalch, Headteacher.

380. Opening of the New Buildings of Highshore School on 30 January 1970.

381. *Southwark Sparrow* 24 May 1991.

382. Brochure to mark the opening of Livesey Museum.

383. Foundation stones of former Nunhead Baptist Church, Gautrey Road.

384. Information provided on 21 January 1993 by the wife of His Eminence Rev. Dr. Prince J. Blackson.

385. Letter dated 18 January 1993 from Cecily Haynes-Hart, Project Co-ordinator, Robert Hart Memorial Supplementary School.

386. Information provided on 23 January 1993 by Cecily Haynes-Hart.

387. *The Apostolic Faith: Its Origin, Functions, and Doctrines.* The Apostolic Faith, Oregon, USA.
388. *The Salvation Army Nunhead Corps Centenary Brochure 1884-1984.*
389. *William Booth* by Minnie Lindsay Carpenter. Wyvern, 1957.
390. *Saint John's Church, Peckham and its inheritance* by Les Mole.
391. *St. John Chrysostom Archbishop of Constantinople* by Les Mole.
392. Letter dated 1 February 1993 from Ron Woollacott.
393. *We the Undersigned...: A History of the Royal London Mutual Insurance Society Limited and its times 1861-1961* by W. Gore Allen. Newman Neame, 1961.
394. Letter dated 3 February 1993 from Miss M. J. Salmon, Property Division, Royal London Asset Management.
395. *S. Saviour's Church, Denmark Park. Jubilee, 1881-1931.*
396. *South London Press* 29 January 1993.
397. Plaque at Kingsbury House.
398. *St. John's, East Dulwich Church and Parish* by Mary Boast. St. John the Evangelist, 1991.
399. Information obtained on 14 February 1993 from Dawn Eckhart, Project Manager.
400. Information obtained from the Environmental Services Department, Southwark Council.
401. London Borough of Southwark Official Guide.
402. Safeway Company History.
403. *Sojourner Truth* by Peter Kraas. Chelsea House Publishers, 1988.
404. Letter dated 19 February 1993 from Mr. J. A. Selkend, Woodhall Developments Ltd.
405. House deeds of 2 Everthorpe Road.
406. Information received in February 1993 from Sojourner Truth Association.
407. *The Macmillan Dictionary of Women's Biography* compiled and edited by Jennifer Uglow. Macmillan, 1989.
408. *Her name was Sojourner Truth* by H. Pauli. 1962.
409. Information provided on 24 January 1993 by a member of Sure Way Christian Centre.
410. Information provided by Stephen C. Humphrey, author of *A Guide to the Archives of Southwark Local Studies Library (1992).*
411. *Southwark Sparrow* 14 May 1993.
412. *South London Press* 14 May 1993.

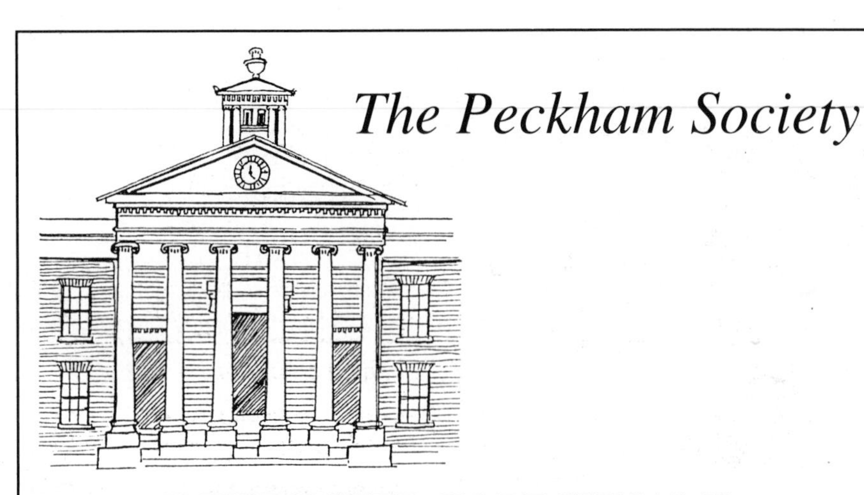

The Peckham Society

INTERESTED IN PECKHAM?
IF SO, YOU WOULD BENEFIT FROM JOINING THE PECKHAM SOCIETY.

This is the amenity society for SE15 and is affiliated to the Civic Trust. It exists to encourage concern for the environment and history of Peckham and the surrounding area.

Illustrated talks and guided tours are arranged.

Committee members attend planning and conservation meetings so the Society can play a full part in determining local issues.

The Peckham Society News is sent free to members. Postcards, maps and books are available.

For more information please contact The Peckham Society at 178 Peckham Rye, SE22 9QA.